THE ART AND SCIENCE OF CULTURE

THE POWER OF SEEING WHAT'S HIDDEN

CHAD CARR, PHD, MBA

MATTHEW HERZBERG, PHD (ABD), MA

Networlding Publishing

ISBN: 978-1-955750-42-4

Networlding PUBLISHING

CONTENTS

PRAISE FOR THE ART AND SCIENCE OF CULTURE

"The hidden elements of culture the authors reveal align with our cultural objectives and would enable any organization to achieve its brand of success."

—GEOFFROY VAN RAEMDONCK, CEO, NEIMAN MARCUS GROUP

"We all know culture drives success in an organization. Chad and Matt bring to life another level of understanding of what creates your culture and help you leverage your culture to unlock your organization's true potential."

—TODD PENEGOR, PRESIDENT & CEO, THE WENDY'S COMPANY

"As a former colleague of Chad and Matt, I've seen firsthand the effect that their systemic approach to culture transformation can have on an organization. From developing a true understanding of your culture to the importance of filling your team with go-to people, these principles are incredibly valuable."

—MIKE THEILMANN, CHRO, ALBERTSONS COMPANIES

"Leadership and culture are keys to sustained financial performance, especially in challenging times. The authors' powerful combination of practical corporate leadership experience with management consulting enables them to reveal those critical culture levers often hidden in firms."

—KEN HANNAH, CFO, CALERES

"Culture has the power to either stall or accelerate business performance. I appreciate how the authors smartly offer insights into both the art and science of aligning strategy and culture to optimize for results."

—STEPHANIE CROOK, VP HR STRATEGY & CULTURE, INTEL

"In the *Art and Science of Culture,* Dr. Carr and Matt Herzberg have blended the science of behavioral change with years of experience helping leaders transform their organizations. The authors have clearly captured the most important drivers of culture as being the collective state of mind throughout the organization. The lessons and experiences described in the book will help any leader or manager engage the principles to shape a healthy, high-performance culture."

—JIM HART, FORMER CEO, SENN DELANEY LEADERSHIP, AND CURRENT CEO, GOME.AI

"The key to long-term growth is to ensure that the culture of an organization supports and aligns with the company's growth strategy. This book provides a very effective model for creating a winning growth culture by understanding what is hidden in an organization and leveraging defined best practices to make the needed changes. Chad and Matt have leveraged their extensive experience to define an easy-to-understand framework with techniques and tools that will create a culture that drives results."

—MARK COSBY, FORMER CEO, MICHAEL'S, AND BOARD MEMBER

"From my perspective as the former CEO of a multinational corporation, and as I now work with CEOs of our portfolio companies, I have witnessed firsthand the power of the ideas and practices that build high-performance organizations across the globe. The systematic approach Matt and Chad deliver creates organizations that sustain themselves over time and routinely beat the competition."

—AHMAD CHATILA, MANAGING PARTNER, FENICE INVESTMENT GROUP

"As a CEO in my third company turnaround, I've lived the deep importance of a vibrant culture to move an organization forward. It's hard, rewarding work, and Chad was a big part of our strategy and execution at Battelle to make that culture change. He and Matt have now taken those lessons to the next level, adding the biological impacts we feel to better prepare leaders to find productive paths forward for their organizations. Peter Drucker was right when he said, "Culture eats strategy for breakfast," and *The Art of Science and Culture* can guide you to improve the culture of your business."

—LOU VON THAER, PRESIDENT & CEO, BATTELLE

"Matt and Chad distill their years of experience and wisdom in leading their own HR organizations and transforming other companies into well-researched, simple ideas that build high-achieving cultures and breakthrough performance."

—SHAKER SADASIVAM, PHD, CEO, AURAGENT BIOSCIENCE

"Transforming leaders from the inside out is key to transforming culture and ultimately driving high levels of sustained performance. Matt and Chad offer deep insights into the neuroscience roots of leadership along with a pragmatic approach for driving meaningful cultural change."

—SUSAN LAMONICA, CHRO & HEAD OF CORPORATE SOCIAL RESPONSIBILITY, CITIZENS FINANCIAL GROUP

"Matt and Chad are experts in the field of guiding leaders through the process of creating and sustaining high performance. This book shares many of their keen insights and meaningful experiences, creating a blueprint for executives."

—HAMMAD SHAH RPH, CEO, CLAREST HEALTH

"During my time in M&A and beyond as an HR leader, I have observed how critical company culture is in creating or destroying value for all stakeholders. Matt and Chad effectively outline the critical leaders' actions required to create and sustain an environment of high performance and healthy corporate culture—making this book a go-to guide for transformation processes."

—BEATRIZ TIELVE, CHIEF PEOPLE & CULTURE OFFICER, X-ELIO

"This book is a must read for anyone who wants a sustainable, high-performance culture that will recruit and retain top talent. Matt and Chad have done a masterful job of explaining not just the art, but also the science of culture change. The book is not just theoretical, either. Matt and Chad provide immensely practical, concrete steps that executives can follow to impact culture and drive results for their companies."

—JAMES R. WEBB, SENIOR VICE PRESIDENT, GENERAL COUNSEL, CHIEF RISK OFFICER & SECRETARY, CONTINENTAL RESOURCES, INC.

"The authors offer deep insights into the neuroscience of leadership and sustainable culture change, which leads to superior performance. I have been able to use the concepts from the book in transforming my leadership team."

—PASHU GOPALAN, CO-CHAIRMAN & CEO, SILRES ENERGY SOLUTIONS PRIVATE LIMITED (INDIA)

"Driving change in an organization is obviously difficult. I want to thank the authors for detailing a framework that provides any leader the ability to positively influence not only their workplace culture, but also their own professional effectiveness and personal satisfaction."

—CHRIS AWAD, PHD, VP OF HUMAN RESOURCES, NEXGEN POWER SYSTEM, INC.

"Savvy investors and leaders have figured out that the path to returns on their financial capital are through attention to and care for the human capital aspects of the organization. There are many books to read on this topic, this one should be on your very short list. Chad and Matt lay out thoughtful *and* pragmatic approaches to creating sustainable value on the truly hard stuff of leadership."

—MICHAEL KEANE, FORMER CHRO PF CHANG'S, BOARD MEMBER, EXECUTIVE COACH & ADVISOR

"*The Art and Science of Culture* is a practical tool for leaders of organizations big and small. By digging into the unseen forces on team culture, Chad and Matt have brought to the surface important conversations and strategies that every leader should be equipped with. My team will benefit from the insights provided in the book as we continue to navigate growth."

—JAMIE SCHISLER, PRESIDENT & CHIEF COMFORT OFFICER, UPWEST

"In this day and age of digital transformation and technology-driven decision making, a CEO's biggest challenge is leading and sometimes pivoting their business strategies to achieve value and growth. Changing and evolving strategies is not the exception—it's the new norm. The difference between doing it successfully or creating a fatal disruption is the culture of the company. Culture is the foundation strategy sits upon. This is the handbook every CEO needs to create that unshakable bedrock upon which strategy can flourish and evolve. Chad and Matt have done an exceptional job of laying out the fundamental and systematic approach to creating the ultimate resilient culture for success."

—MARY KAY O'CONNOR-WENTE, FORMER CEO, TEK BRANDS, BOARD MEMBER

"*The Art and Science of Culture* provides a pragmatic playbook for all C-suite leaders and is an especially invaluable resource for chief executives and chief HR officers who seek to accelerate culture transformation. The engaging content, practical pointers, and "from the coalface" examples make this a thoughtful and rewarding read. Bravo to Chad Carr and Matt Herzberg for so eloquently demystifying culture and producing my new go-to guide on organizational culture."

—SUSAN STEELE, CHIEF PEOPLE OFFICER, EBIQUITY

"All organizations want a culture that creates sustained success and superior outcomes, but doing this is difficult. Matt and Chad's knowledge and experience in the book provide great insights and a roadmap to build and maintain a high-performing culture. I appreciate their deep understanding of the science of culture change, along with the practical tools and methodologies they provide. A great and valuable read."

—MARK LINDGREN, SVP, CORPORATE COMMUNICATIONS & CHRO OF AMEREN

"Culture is the key ingredient that defines success or failure for all companies. It's critical that all leaders align their culture to the company strategy, nurture it, and embody these qualities. This book provides valuable insights into the art and science of culture using real-world case studies. The authors provide a proven process of building strong cultural values along with a scalable framework that your organization can easily understand, take to heart, and adopt. Building a rich culture will lead your organization to superior performance and higher customer value, and will enrich employees' lives."

—RON MCCUTCHEN, VP, NVIDIA

"This book has much to offer C-suite executives as they go about the critical task of creating culture and leading change within their organizations. I can't emphasize enough leadership's role in defining and modeling the desired culture. The effort is doomed to fail when that role is abdicated elsewhere (especially to HR). In my many years of leading HR, I find that most employees *want* to do a good job, but the hidden elements within the organization's culture prevent success. Matt and Chad have done an exceptional job of utilizing both research and their significant practical experience to simplify the concept of culture and shed light on the hidden elements that impede business results. Most importantly, this book provides leaders with an easy-to-understand road map, practical tools, and on-point questions they can use tomorrow to create a healthier, more nimble culture—a must-read for all executives."

—MELANIE CURTIS, CHRO, LAIRD CONNECTIVITY, INC.

"In the crowded landscape of cultural transformation, the benefit of an iterative, systematic approach that enables an organization to reap the business impact of a high-performing culture is often missing. In *The Art and Science of Culture,* Chad and Matt provide a well-researched, practical, and intentional guide for leaders and organizations to maximize their results through continuous reflection and improvement. Regardless of where you are in your culture journey, this book provides the framework for improving success for your people and your organization."

—SEAN DINEEN, CHIEF PEOPLE OFFICER, ADVANCED CALL CENTER TECHNOLOGIES

"If toxic behavior in a workplace is left unchecked, it will spread to the entire organization. Leaders must nurture their teams so that they can build a strong culture that drives positive results. Chad and Matt show you how to never take culture for granted. Listen, observe, and ask lots of questions to develop a strong and resilient culture."

—MEGAN HERNANDEZ, FORMER SVP OF STORES, EXPRESS

"Culture drives company performance and it is critical in creating an environment of trust. In the world of private equity, it is common to see transactions where a merger of equals creates an enormous opportunity to generate shareholder return. Ultimately the ability of leadership to navigate the complex process of culture building will either make or break the investment thesis. Matt and Chad provide a well-thought-out playbook for culture building and driving performance."

—KEITH CLINE, CEO, CEA STUDY ABROAD & CAPA: THE GLOBAL EDUCATION NETWORK

"We build—or degrade—culture by what we say (words) and what we do (behaviors). This is a powerful resource for any leader looking to explore, understand, and shape culture in a pragmatic and results-oriented manner."

—JEN HINKLE, CHRO, ARHAUS

"Chad and Matt catapult traditional culture theory into the present day with powerful lessons that are timely and relevant. They seamlessly synthesize perspectives from the macro environment, discoveries in neuroscience, and their own research in real-life corporate settings. Their wisdom is like rocket fuel, capable of transforming others both personally and professionally.

—CHAROLETTE OBRINGER, GROUP VICE PRESIDENT, BELK

Foreword by Tom Peters

Let me begin my commentary with two stories…

Story #1: I call it "epiphany day," much as I don't like that overused word. It occurred in mid-1977, when I had more or less just begun the research that led, four years later, to *In Search of Excellence.* My future co-author, Bob Waterman, and I worked in McKinsey & Company's San Francisco office, and we had a date, 30 miles south in Palo Alto, with HP president John Young.

You must understand that we worked on the 50th floor of the Bank of America Center—the Big Guys' office area two floors above us was occupied by armies of executive assistants and featured tea-service china that would not have been out of place in Buckingham Palace. So, it was a surprising start to our HP visit when John Young, the president of the then $1 billion company, came out to the front desk to greet Bob and me and take us to his 8-foot-by-8-foot cubicle with half walls.

Midway through our conversation that epiphany occurred, though I wouldn't label it that way for many years. John introduced us to the "HP Way." Call it "the way we do things around here" or "management style"—those were the standard terms for what today we call "corporate culture," a phrase not in the management thesaurus in the late 1970s.

Explaining HP's approach, John further introduced us to MBWA, or Managing by Wandering Around, the centerpiece of the HP Way. Leadership was not an office or meeting room thing at HP, it was an "out and about with the folks who do the real work" thing. It meant just that: wandering around. For guys like Bob and me, who were used to working with Bank of America, it was, yes, that epiphany, the idea that leading, even in a big company, could be hands-on, informal, and intimate.

I must add that, toward the end of the visit, John took Bob and me around, and along the way, we ran into an old fellow chatting about some new product issue with a 25-year-old engineer in front of a computer screen; the old chap to whom we were introduced was, uh, Bill Hewlett. My whole model of leadership and communication and the way-we-do-things-around-here/corporate culture was turned upside down that day. HP, with its giantism, has, alas, lost much of its magic, as most giants do, but on that day in 1977, it was sparkling and intimate and alive.

Story #2: I call this one "getting even day" (really "revenge day," but that's a horrible word). My research in 1977–1980 had what we now call corporate culture as its centerpiece. That notion did not sit well with the strategy-first-by-the-numbers crowd at the tiptop of McKinsey's pecking order. In particular, it bugged the hell out of senior partner Lou Gerstner.

But Bob and I stuck to our guns and *In Search of Excellence* featured it—and to our surprise and delight, the book sold relatively well. Lou left McKinsey and after a couple of stops earned his sky-high, well-deserved, front-cover reputation by turning a sluggish IBM around about 180 degrees.

Lou wrote about his IBM foray in a book-memoir titled *Who Says Elephants Can't Dance? Inside IBM's Historic Turnaround.* He reports at one point on what he called his premier "lesson learned": "If I could have chosen not to tackle the IBM culture head on, I probably wouldn't have. My bias coming in was toward strategy, analysis, and measurement. In comparison, changing hundreds of thousands of people's attitudes and behaviors is very hard. Yet I came to see in my time at IBM that culture isn't just one aspect of the game—it is *the* game." When I read those words—"it is *the* game"—I laughed so hard I cried, and I immediately called Bob so we could gloat together.

All of this storytelling is a way of explaining why I love this book, *The Art and Science of Culture: The Power of Seeing What's Hidden*. Culture, I believe and have preached for over forty years, "is *the* game." And this to me is the best guide imaginable for telling practitioners just what culture is, how to dig under the covers and analyze it ("see what's hidden"), and modify it to achieve that "excellence" I have written about in nineteen books.

This book is staggeringly well-researched. I was bowled over, for example, by some of the hard science that allows us to truly understand what does go on beneath the covers (and between the ears) of those who toil in and lead organizations. I am an avid—obsessive is actually the correct word—reader, and I can say that among the many books on the topic of corporate culture I've ingested, this one dives the deepest into the process of understanding and changing an organization's culture. I could call it a "page turner" (it was for me), but it really demands deep study to appreciate the neurological roots of "what's hidden" in the heads of the folks who work for and with you.

Read.
Study.
Study some more.
And then get to work.
It is the game.

INTRODUCTION

Through our years working in the field of culture transformation, with company after company, leader after leader, executive team after executive team, we have heard the same challenges in statements such as:

- "My organization isn't accountable."
- "My executive team members are too focused on their functions or divisions. They aren't thinking about what's best for the whole organization."
- "We are not aligned on the critical priorities for the organization."
- "We need innovation and growth, but people won't act or take risks."
- "We're growing so fast, we are losing our sense of a shared culture."

Even though we had collectively spent decades working at the top of some of the world's largest publicly traded and privately held firms and completed 23 years of formal education between us in the fields of business, education, psychology, and organization theory, we just couldn't see what was *hidden*.

Additionally, during all our years in the field, we worked for organizations that spent millions upon millions of dollars and countless hours trying to drive transformations in companies only to be met with constant resistance to change. Even when the CEO was visibly committed to a change, we would still find it very difficult to align the organization to its new expectations.

We heard similar statements regarding improving culture. Basically, we couldn't see the water we were swimming in. We couldn't understand why people behaved the way they did—why they would throw others under the proverbial business-as-usual bus (and why we would do the same). But eventually, we began to see both an *art* and *science of* organizational culture emerging, including its *obvious* and, even more importantly, its *hidden* elements.

We discovered the power of the *role of thought* at play in every one of these cultures. As a result of our discovery of these hidden elements, we were able to succeed where we were previously met with constant roadblocks. So, what was this change?

THE HIDDEN ELEMENTS OF THOUGHT AND NEUROSCIENCE

Our focus was originally on the obvious things: the observable behaviors; communications; and how we selected, developed, trained, rewarded, and built talent in high-performance organizations. But through our research and discovery, we realized we were missing the *hidden factors*—factors that turned out to be essential to achieving rapid, effective, and sustainable change.

The more we looked, the more we began to see just how much was hidden from us in everyday business conversations, not just in our discussions with leaders and teams, but at large, for everybody. We realized that the *role of thought was rarely discussed and rarely explored.* Additionally, we saw that each of us has a set of underlying ideas—more specifically, thought habits and beliefs—that strongly influence how we behave in an organization, day in and day out.

At the same time, we were applying what we learned about the *role of thought,* and the neuroscience movement was exploding. The deep insights gleaned from this movement helped us to understand further how our brains physically rewire themselves as we learn and how *mirror neurons,* embedded in our brains, help us detect and model behaviors after those around us.

In the process of our discovery, what had been hidden from us for decades became clear. As a result of our findings, we began to understand what we've come to call *the art and science of culture.*

WE ARE ALL HUMAN—AND ACT ACCORDINGLY

From the balcony view we've been privileged to have, cultures look much the same across clients, geographies, and industries. As we have gratefully become able to see what was once hidden, we now know there is a remarkable consistency in the challenges of human beings working with other human beings.

We see the many issues that arise around accountability, alignment, safety, collaboration, inclusion, risk-taking, and innovation. These consistencies suggest that underlying *(hidden)* realities exist within your culture and every culture. These realities seem to be simply an element of human nature that we all experience as we work together in complex organizations.

We have delved even further over the years into *why* it doesn't make sense for leaders and employees to act in any of the sub-optimal ways we've recounted above. However, we eventually found hidden reasons that explain why their actions make perfect sense *to them*. For example, one key insight we've discovered is that, for whatever reason, companies tend not to focus on or may not even have thought about those hidden reasons.

We also firmly believe that we act in ways that make sense to us, given our current state of mind. So, when we understand why it makes sense to act the way we are today, we can explore that thinking and the hardwiring in our brains that perpetuates positive and negative behaviors. This is why the key to transforming cultures starts with personal transformation.

In this book, we will point out many of the hidden reasons you may not be aware of that prevent you from developing your ideal culture. We are confident that by the end of this book you will be able to unlock your full potential to create your winning culture.

Our goal is to provide you with illuminating change and growth techniques along with tools that are versatile that will help you tackle almost any cultural challenge. So, let's get started.

ARE THERE TIMES WHEN YOU DON'T KNOW WHAT YOU DON'T KNOW?

This is the question that started us on our journey of discovery, and it will help you start down the same path to improve your culture. This is the critical intersection where you realize you don't know what you don't know. Getting to that intersection involves a significant challenge. It requires adopting a beginner's mindset or a *whatever-it-takes* determination with both *curiosity* and *humility*. No matter what, it's about taking a new approach to an old problem—that of changing your culture for the better.

To further accelerate learning the art and science of culture by discovering the *hidden* elements, we will:

- Offer a straightforward, practical, and complete illumination of organizational cultures, starting with what is hidden for most leaders.
- Share stories that illuminate the most significant culture-change issues we have seen.
- Reveal the patterns we've discovered by sharing comprehensive frameworks and real-life examples.
- Provide a method to help you not only ask the right questions, but also follow a proven process for discovering your own hidden elements.
- Deliver a comprehensive overview of what we've learned from our direct experience in leading transformational culture changes *from the inside* and *outside of* some of the world's most admired companies as we worked with hundreds of executive, division, and functional leadership teams.
- Draw on our practical experience and emerging research in human behavior and neuroscience.
- Integrate our lessons learned with the timeless principles of transformational change.

Our goal is simple: to help you get a clear picture of building an awe-inspiring culture within your organization to unleash optimal business results.

BEGINNING TO SEE THE HIDDEN PATTERNS OF CULTURE WITHIN YOUR ORGANIZATION

Building an awe-inspiring culture involves recognizing the patterns inherent in cultures, especially those hidden from our awareness. Herbert Simon of Carnegie Mellon University wrote an article entitled, "Making Management Decisions: The Role of Intuition and Emotion."[1] The article reviewed a body of research exploring how leaders make decisions effectively and efficiently.

Simon cites an experiment involving both grandmaster and novice chess players. In this experiment, both groups were shown a real but unfamiliar chess game involving 25 pieces. Participants were also shown the game for only 10 seconds and then asked to recreate the position of the pieces on the board. On average, grandmasters were able to place 23 to 24 pieces on the correct squares. In contrast, novice players were only able to place five or six pieces on the right squares.

In the first review of this experiment, one might conclude that the grandmaster chess players had incredible cognitive ability in memory and spatial reasoning. To test this observation further, a second study was conducted. In that study, 25 chess pieces were randomly placed on a chessboard. After a 10-second viewing, the novice players could only place 5 or 6 pieces correctly on the board. However, the remarkable thing was that the *grandmasters could only correctly put five or six pieces* on the board. That is, it was not a real game.

Simon concluded that the grandmasters' success in the earlier experiment had less to do with their cognitive ability and more about their ability to *recognize patterns* within an established game. The grandmasters understood the rules and structures within the game while the novice players did not. The implications for leaders in organizations are very similar. Suppose leaders can see and understand the patterns of successful relationship building and other patterns that result in cultural transformations. In that case, they can use them to effect change in positive and productive ways.

Throughout this book, we will help you begin to see patterns in your culture that are common in most of the organizations we have helped transform. For example, leaders used to operating in *command and control* are disappointed that their teams are not more *empowered*. Yet, when asked, their people will tell you that they don't get to make any of the real decisions anyway—so they wait for the leader to make the decisions. By shifting a small leadership behavior toward delegating a few more decisions, leaders can see dramatic changes in empowerment in their organizations.

CULTURE'S ROLE IN YOUR FUTURE OF WORK

As we prepare to publish this book, there has been a growing urgency in preparing for the "future of work." This is a tremendous change for some firms— moving to hybrid work models, tapping into automation, managing anxiety, and learning how to lead and manage cultures remotely. For other firms, the future of work requires just a few adjustments from past practices. Firms leverage things like cloud-based knowledge management systems, virtual decision-making platforms, artificial intelligence–based coaching, virtual and augmented reality experiences, and virtual and in-person participation in meetings to get work done and develop future leaders.

Regardless of the scope of change you are anticipating, culture will continue to play a critical role in your organization, thus substantially impacting how you manage your culture and how you may need to adapt *your* future of work. The models and principles we discuss here are not bound by factors like in-person versus hybrid, workforce automation, employee well-being, or remotely leading teams. And, importantly, the core concepts around aligning teams, developing shared symbols and language, and developing healthy *states of mind* will become even more critical in your future of work.

Once you begin to become aware of the current culture operating in your organization and feel the energy you get when it aligns with your strategy, you will consistently *choose* to shape it to drive results.

THE IMPORTANCE OF NOTICING AND CONSIDERING

As we do this work with senior teams worldwide, we start by asking them just to notice *and consider*. We'll ask you to do the same. Throughout the book, we will explore concepts typically *hidden* from our view. We will ask you to notice how these things show up for you. Do they make sense? Have you seen them in your organization? Do others seem to notice them? Or are they currently hidden? Once you notice them, we ask you to consider the impact of trying some of our recommendations. For example, we may suggest that changing the way you ask questions can create higher levels of innovation and creativity in your organization. Don't take our word for it. Consider it for yourself. Does it make sense? Would it be worth trying it out to assess the impact?

As you apply these principles, we expect you to find how they show up and operate in your life and in your workplace. It's not so important exactly how we describe our experience with them. It's really up to you to notice and consider how these may show up and operate for you.

HOW TO USE THIS BOOK

As you think about how to get the most out of this book, we reflect on the advice once shared by Sir Francis Bacon: "Some books are to be tasted, others to be swallowed, and some few to be chewed and digested." The same can be said about the chapters that follow. Depending on your needs, you may want to sample and focus on key areas, such as how to drive culture transformation or how cultures really work. For others, you will find that carefully considering all the concepts presented throughout the book repeatedly will deepen your understanding of culture and how to cultivate the culture you really want in your organization.

In either case, we have prepared *key takeaways* from each chapter and *questions to consider* as you think about how to apply the concepts to enhance your organization's culture. In the end, we created this book to help illuminate what has been hidden, to demystify what corporate culture really is and to rapidly reshape it to unleash your performance.

CHAPTER 1
WHY ARE CEOS PAYING ATTENTION TO CULTURE?

Culture constrains strategy.

EDGAR SCHEIN

For decades, researchers have documented culture's impact on company performance. In 1982, Tom Peters and Robert Waterman studied what made the most successful American companies successful.[1] In it, they found eight characteristics of excellent companies:

- A bias for action
- Staying close to the customer
- Autonomy and entrepreneurship
- Productivity through people
- Hands-on, value-driven
- Stick to the knitting
- Simple form, lean staff
- Simultaneous loose-tight properties

In brief, they found that the *soft* elements of companies were *hard* but also *critical* to a company's success.

In 1992, in a groundbreaking study, James Heskett and John Kotter looked at the corporate cultures of approximately 200 companies over 11 years and documented their impact on financial performance. They found that companies with strong organizational cultures increased:[2]

- Net income by over 756 percent compared to companies lacking in culture, which grew by only 1 percent.
- Stock prices by 901 percent versus 74 percent in companies lacking culture.
- Revenue by 682 percent versus 166 percent.
- Employee growth by 282 percent versus 36 percent.

Over the past 30 years, this link between culture and performance has been supported repeatedly in academic and consulting research. [3] It is why, increasingly, management teams, boards, and now even regulators and shareholders are taking a greater interest in the topic of culture.

HUMAN CAPITAL AND CULTURE'S IMPACT ON FIRM VALUATION

Approximately 85 percent of a typical organization's costs are tied to people, so it makes sense to consider the productivity and capabilities of those people when valuing firms. In fact, in a recent conversation with a CEO of a privately held firm, she shared that a private equity firm identified her culture as a significant factor in the valuation of her firm.

On August 26, 2020, the U.S. Securities and Exchange Commission issued a rule that fundamentally changed how organizations disclose material information, requiring disclosures around human capital. Human capital elements go beyond reporting headcount and basic employee statistics, even in publicly traded companies. In the past, companies had to report *only one* human capital metric: the number of employees. The new rule requires reporting the number of employees, but also requires more clarity with other reporting requirements.

Most importantly, though, for the first time, companies are required to include any human capital measure or description of human capital resources, including metrics and objectives the business focuses on in managing their business. This includes attraction, development, and retention of talent. And these are just the table stakes. Many of our clients see their culture as an *asset* and report on cultural health using measures such as employee engagement, contribution to innovation, psychological safety, or broader culture measures.

As investors begin to ask for these measurements, top management teams are considering how to report key culture-related metrics, especially when this conversation has entered the business vernacular, and it can be demonstrated that the health of the culture adds to economic value.

THE IMPACT OF CULTURE ON PERFORMANCE CAN BE ENORMOUS

What follows are two cautionary tales; examples we hope will awaken in you a desire to know your culture better than you do today and to take measured steps to improve it.

A culture that discouraged bad news

In 2002, GM first detected an ignition switch defect during pre-production testing of the Saturn Ion. In subsequent years, GM approved the use of the defective ignition switch supplied by a company called Delphi, even though it did not meet GM's own performance specifications.

Repeatedly, engineers flagged the ignition switch issue, but the company rejected multiple proposals to fix the problem because it would take too long and cost too much. By 2005, reports of stalling vehicles and fatal crashes involving a faulty airbag had been reported. Sadly however, it was not until *February 2014* that GM finally recalled the defective ignition switch that was causing these problems.[4]

Why did it take nearly ten years to deal with a defective part knowingly installed into millions of cars? Federal investigators believe that GM's *corporate culture discouraged discussion of bad news*, a problem exacerbated by the pressure of the 2008 financial crisis and the act of taxpayers bailing out the company.

The cost and consequences of a low-trust culture were incredibly high. All told, there were countless lives lost and more than $4.1 billion paid by GM in settlements and recall costs for a fix that would have cost just 90 cents per switch while the cars were in production.

"Paralyzed with fear"

Especially since the COVID-19 pandemic, organizations are turning to digital transformation to allow them to reach customers remotely. There is no question that improving one's culture is an essential enabler of digital transformation.

This commitment to culture change became the charge of the chief information officer (we'll call her Mary) in a global technology company we worked with at one point. Here, Mary was committed to developing an agile approach to managing technology projects inside the company. After McKinsey set the strategy and Accenture helped create the organization design and systems, Mary launched the new agile approach within her 7,000-person global IT organization.

But as a few months passed, Mary noticed that agile wasn't happening. Employees were still risk-averse to the new approach. They continued to manage their projects as they always had—slowly, methodically, and carefully using the waterfall method. Feeling frustrated, Mary *insisted* that the organization move more quickly, to iterate, and take some risks.

However, sensing Mary's frustration, employees became even more reluctant to step out of line or try something new for fear of failure. In this case, as in many similar ones, the culture was stuck in the past, frozen in unproductive behaviors, so deeply embedded they could be called unconscious.

Why? For decades, the IT leaders and team members were rewarded for their behaviors of carefully planning, executing, and controlling projects using industry-standard project management tools. They had literally hardwired their brains to methodically track risks and mitigate them, keep things on plan, and regularly monitor and adjust their projects to achieve results.

There were countless stories of former employees who failed to adapt to an agile framework and, as a result, were forced to exit the company. Each of their past promotions and even bonuses rewarded their ability to control and minimize risks to the organization.

It wasn't until a year down the road that the CIO commissioned a study of the culture of their global 7,000-person IT organization only to find out that their employees were "paralyzed with fear." All that they had learned over decades to do was no longer welcome and yet, they did not feel it was safe to take the risks that would be required to run an agile organization.

The failure to focus on their culture shift to an agile workplace during the larger transformation set back the execution of their strategy by over 18 months. And in today's organizations, 18 months can be the majority of the CIO's tenure.

REALIZE THAT EVERY ORGANIZATION HAS SOME LEVEL OF DYSFUNCTION

Every organization is dysfunctional at times. Employees don't collaborate when they should, allow projects to fail even when they know how to make them successful, or blame others even when they realize they share accountability. Or worse, strategic, ethical, or financial lapses occur that end up costing organizations their reputations, significant profits, or, in the worst-case scenario, their very existence (e.g., Lehman Bros., Enron, Theranos, Arthur Andersen, Borders).

The accumulation of these types of cultural behaviors, such as low levels of accountability, lack of teamwork and agility, and low levels of innovation, can directly impact your organization's ability to thrive, and to generate results. Imagine having an entire organization of people who behave as some at GM behaved over this ten-year period. Even though this is an extreme example, it becomes easy to understand the direct impact that culture has on your results.

DEVELOPING AN ORGANIZATION FULL OF GO-TO PEOPLE

Dysfunction costs organizations billions of dollars per year. For example, on February 5, 2018, Wells Fargo lost $29 billion in market capitalization in a single day, after the company was penalized by the Federal Reserve because the reserve could "not tolerate pervasive and persistent misconduct at any bank."[5]

Conversely, companies listed among the best places to work based on their corporate culture had 20 percent higher returns to shareholders than comparable companies over a five-year period.[6] CEOs are becoming increasingly aware of both the potential risks *and the upsides* of managing culture.

Instead of imagining a dysfunctional organization, bring to mind a go-to person on your team. You can count on this person to tackle any challenge and to successfully achieve results. Now, imagine a whole organization filled with go-to people. Let's now explore the value and the opportunity of building such an organization.

Several years ago, we were helping a large shipping company improve the cultural health of their operating division. After aligning the senior team, we worked with the broader organization to help them bring their values to life—to embed their ideal culture. As part of our work, we formed a culture leadership team that would be responsible not only for ensuring that the culture stayed healthy, but also for measuring the impact of that healthy culture on operating results.

Quarter after quarter, we would regroup as a team and look at the operating metrics and how they compared to the company's historical-operating performance. As we explored third-quarter results, the organization found that, for the first time in 40 years, it had outperformed its operating plan for 43 consecutive weeks. This included lower damaged goods returns, more on-time deliveries, and even lower instances of employees calling off from work.

The bottom line? The senior team acknowledged that working on their culture, which they had once thought was the "soft stuff," produced significant, measurable hard results.

CULTURE DRIVES RESULTS

If you imagine an entire organization made up of more and more culture-focused, go-to people, you will see results like those we have observed in organizations that develop high-performing cultures:

- EBITDA more than two-and-a-half times higher
- Revenue seven times higher
- Turnover reduced by 60 percent
- Ability to hire ideal candidates increased by 40 percent
- Increased innovation, inclusion, and belonging

Another example: We were six months into a culture engagement for a large consumer company. We began to see a positive shift in the spirit of the organization. Coinciding with this shift, we also saw an inflection point showing a shift toward revenue and stock price growth.

The great news is that this company sustained its growth for over four years, generating historical high watermarks time and again. Meanwhile, during the same period, they had year after year of statistically significant improvements in all culture measures.

While we can never completely establish the impact of culture change alone, CEOs and other leaders tell us that culture plays a big part in delivering their remarkable results. To explore this notion more fully, let's look at two different ways of operating within a team or an organization. One which we'll call "lower performing." The other, as we referenced earlier, we call "go-to."

The lower-performing organization tends to sub-optimize its results. On the other hand, the go-to organization not only meets its goals, but exceeds them.

Figure 1.1 shows some of the behaviors you might witness in organizations when they are not functioning at their best. Here, you may hear statements such as, "That's the way we've always done it," or "They don't get it," or "That's not my job." All too often, these statements are indicative of negative attitudes that we witness playing out time and time again. When you hear this type of language, it suggests that your people are *off their game.*

Figure 1.1 How culture impacts results through unhealthy states of mind.

THE HIDDEN REASONS WE ARE SOMETIMES OFF OUR GAME

Neuroscience is the key to understanding and addressing what is happening when employees are off their game. It's about looking at what's going on in their brains. What author Daniel Goleman called the *amygdala hijack,*[7] we refer to simply as an *amygdala trip.* Like an electrical circuit breaker can be tripped and take a circuit offline, the amygdala can trip and shut off power to the ability to reason, exercise judgment, and innovate.

In our view, the word *hijack* indicates something done to us by someone else. And yet, our experience is that we get to choose whether or not we trip the breaker ourselves. For example, imagine being in a large meeting with a senior leader presenting some significant news about the company's future. Not everyone would have their amygdala hijacked. Only some would trip, based on how they perceive the change. In other words, one person may be excited about the news while another may be anxious and worried (with a tripped amygdala).

The amygdala is a collection of neurons deep in the temporal lobe within the limbic system. The term *amygdala* comes from the Latin word for almond, which is shaped similarly.

As a result of an *amygdala trip*, the amygdala immediately shuts down the neural pathways to the prefrontal cortex—making it very difficult to reason or act rationally.

When we have a fearful response to something, the amygdala sends signals to the hypothalamus, releasing two primary chemicals: adrenaline and cortisol.[8] These chemicals divert blood and oxygen away from thinking centers and into action centers. This response happens so fast that we unaware of it in our conscious minds. Our conscious thinking occurs only *after* the body has already responded! In other words, the amygdala recognizes fear before the cerebral cortex.

Further reactions include significant reductions in the ability to make complex decisions and consider multiple perspectives. As a result, attention narrows, and we find ourselves trapped in the one perspective that makes us feel the safest: "I'm right and you're wrong." In effect, our thinking becomes unreliable.

FIGHT, FLIGHT, OR FREEZE

Our hard-wired behavioral choices include *fight* or *flight.* We see a third option in most organizations when it is impossible to *fight* or *take flight*— and that is to *freeze.* We have run into this phenomenon time and again during large transformation initiatives. Here, people tend to keep their heads down and wait, which drags down the pace of transformation dramatically until people feel the psychological safety to re-engage. In fact, in a recent meeting, a key second-level leader with a 30-year tenure in a large organization said she was going to "wait this out" when speaking about a CEO who was making changes that were not in the best interest of the organization, in her opinion.

This dangerous intersection can delay or completely derail your change effort. Psychological safety is about maintaining a healthy state of mind so we can apply judgment, collaborate, and make effective decisions. And not allowing the amygdala to trip.

HEALTHY CULTURES COME NATURALLY WHEN WE ARE *AT OUR BEST*

In contrast, as Figure 1.2 shows, when employees are able to perform at their best, they can more easily become go-to people in a team or organization. In this case, you will hear employees ask or say things like, "How can I help?" "What support do you need?" or "Let's try this...." Imagine the cumulative effects of having more and more go-to people in your organization.

Figure 1.2 How culture impacts results through healthy states of mind.

Can you relate to comments within each of these types of organizations? Have you spent time in the lower-performing mindset as well as time in the go-to mindset? As a leader, you wouldn't be where you are if you weren't seen as a go-to performer. And, yet, you can likely recall times where you instead showed up with a lower-performing mindset.

Beginning to notice which mindset you show up with is an important capability that we will discuss throughout this book as it is a necessary precursor to developing the culture you want. This powerful science of the mind shows us that as we increase our personal awareness, we can more reliably choose the behaviors we want—behaviors that will drive improved performance.

THE HIDDEN REASONS WHY WE ARE AT OUR BEST

Neuroscience teaches us that when we are *at our best,* we experience higher levels of dopamine, serotonin, and oxytocin:[9]

- Dopamine increases our alertness.
- Serotonin regulates our state of mind to be more positive.
- Oxytocin reduces pain perception and increases our emotional connection with others.

When we feel at our best, we don't activate our amygdala and therefore we avoid the amygdala trip. As a result, the part of our brain that is active against negative emotions like fear is not triggered. Instead, we can create a proactive culture growth environment with all employees using healthy mindsets like curiosity, teamwork, and innovation.

THE IMPACT OF ALIGNING CULTURE TO YOUR STRATEGY

If you as a leader can show up at your best, you can begin to deliberately align your actions to generate the most valued results in your organization. As you think about leveraging culture to improve your firm's performance, consider how to align it to your unique strategy to win in the market. The key to winning in the market is to then align your systems, culture, and high-performance work practices to support your strategy, as shown in Figure 1.3.

Figure 1.3 When you align culture to strategy, structure, and high-performance work practices, your organization will outperform.

THE WORLD CHANGES

We see in most organizations the *ability* to adapt strategy to quickly address changes in markets. Once they refine their strategy to be more competitive, they quickly turn to reorganizing and integrating their people and systems to better align with their strategy. To increase innovation, they may hire a chief innovation officer or change reporting relationships. They may also look to create internal incubation labs to rapidly develop and test new ideas to be deployed.

However, what organizations often neglect, as we shared earlier, is aligning their culture to these new demands. For example, trying to drive *innovation* within a *risk-averse culture* can be frustrating and debilitating. Building a *consistent global brand* in an organization that was once mainly sub-brands, with a culture that de-emphasized *teamwork,* will be slow to achieve. Figure 1.4 illustrates the lag that happens when strategies shift without aligning culture.

Figure 1.4 As the world changes, we adapt to survive by adjusting the obvious things: strategy, structure, and work practices. Still, hidden culture often lags, leading to misalignment and resistance in the organization.

HOW DO YOU SYSTEMATICALLY ALIGN CULTURE WITH STRATEGY?

One clear example of this alignment of strategy, structure, culture, and work practices is the case of a division of a large medical instruments manufacturing company. This division had recently appointed a new president. The charge from the CEO was very clear: double the size of the business from $2 billion to $4 billion in a three-year period while maintaining and even improving margins. The president contacted us and relayed his need to build collaboration and trust in his team.

The first step of the journey was to align senior management. This included alignment around their noble purpose, their values, their business priorities, and the culture that they wanted to create to dramatically grow the business. After several months of reflection and dialogue, the leadership team, with the strong participation and support of the president, focused its efforts on building the culture to encourage an environment of gratitude, curiosity, and accountability.

Next, the senior leadership team engaged the next level of leadership, which was about 250 people. Special emphasis was placed on the need for leaders to be grateful, curious, and accountable in order to engage employees and meet the growth goals.

A culture task force composed of several members of the senior leadership team and several key high potentials from the next level of leadership was enlisted to draft an impactful and robust culture plan. This plan included a comprehensive communication campaign about the culture transformation for the organization, a method and process to engage every employee in the division, and a compelling set of key metrics.

The metrics contained quantifiable measures of human capital, operational, and financial effectiveness. The human capital measures included levels of gratitude, curiosity, and accountability in the organization as captured in their annual employee engagement and culture surveys. The operating measures were a reduction in the cycle time for research and development, growth in sales especially in Europe, and successful integration of acquisitions. The financial metrics included growth in revenue (doubling in three years) and maintaining margins.

Once the culture plan had been developed, the attention turned to engaging the entire organization worldwide, with a special focus on the sales team, since sales were critical to the growth of the business. As we worked through the sales organization, one of the sales leaders realized that the structure of the sales force and the incentive pay program was detrimental to the organization's long-term growth.

This sales leader took it upon himself to work with the head of sales and human resources to restructure sales territories and sales positions and to revamp the sales compensation systems. This restructuring was critical to reaching the growth goal. In fact, the division president commented, "In retrospect, without this change in the sales organization, reaching our growth goal of $4 billion would have been impossible."

Further, he said, "Without the strong focus on increasing trust levels and improving the health of the culture, even suggesting changes to the sales structure much less pay plans would have been impossible. This work paid off."

As this organization increased employee engagement; raised general levels of gratitude, curiosity, and accountability; reduced the R&D cycle time; increased sales in Europe; and successfully integrated several acquisitions, revenue increased to $4 billion while maintaining margins.

As you can see, culture can constrain strategy or accelerate the value an organization can create. The important thing is to begin to notice the culture in action—in yourself and those around you. The more time you spend at your best and intentionally aligning your actions to support your strategy, the more value you create. In the next chapter, we will share a framework to help illuminate the *hidden* elements of culture that primarily account for how people act in your organization.

KEY TAKEAWAYS

- Left unchecked, culture can derail major transformational initiatives.
- Culture is always acting on your organization, whether or not you are aware of it.
- Enabling your employees to be at their best more often equips them to notice their actions and choose to align them with your vision.
- Aligning your culture to your strategy will accelerate your business results.

QUESTIONS TO CONSIDER

- What has changed in your markets, your strategy, or your organization that will require new patterns of behavior in your culture?
- Which behaviors do you see in your organization that can be barriers to high performance?
- What behaviors are most critical to enabling your strategy?
- What specific value can you unlock by building a go-to organization, full of healthy states of mind?
- What is one thing you can do currently to align your culture with your strategy?

CHAPTER 2
A FRAMEWORK FOR THE ART AND SCIENCE OF CULTURE

Soft is hard.

TOM PETERS

For decades, Tom Peters has helped us learn how hard it can be to put people first, shape cultures, and lead with all of the other "soft" stuff. Most leaders are focused on the hard things, like results, profits, operations. In fact, Peters's work has in many ways defined "excellence" and contributed to the tremendous growth in the culture industry.[1]

What we have found in doing culture transformation work for decades is that shaping cultures *is* hard—until you begin to see what is *hidden*. As we said in the previous chapter, what was hidden from us for years is the role that thinking plays in our lives and how that generates our state of mind.

This chapter lays out a framework for understanding culture that includes noticing your state of mind and other hidden elements that have become more obvious to us over time. We've worked on culture transformation inside and on behalf of some of the world's most admired organizations. We share a simple way of looking at a culture that can help you both make sense of it and transform it.

Much like gardening, cultures grow and evolve whether we tend to them, or not. The choice is really about whether we plan, cultivate, and monitor our culture intentionally to align with our strategy or whether we just let it grow unchecked.

WHAT IS CULTURE, REALLY?

Culture is always operating in your company. It's how people do every single task—from strategic planning to customer experience, from rewards to performance management. Every order you take, the engagement you deliver is created by leveraging your culture. It's how you achieve every win. It also contributes to every loss.

So, what is organizational *culture*?

- "A system of publicly and collectively accepted meaning operating for a given group at a given time."[2]
- "A sociocultural system of strategies and practices."[3]
- "Shared perceptions of organizational work practices."[4]
- "Sets of symbols and myths."[5]
- "Shared attitudes and practices."[6]

In our experience, Edgar Schein, professor emeritus of Work and Organization Studies at MIT and one of the leading sociologists of the workplace, offers one of the most complete and valuable definitions of culture. He defines it this way:

> Culture is a pattern of shared basic assumptions that the group learned as it solved its problems of external adaptation and internal integration, that has worked well enough to be considered valid and, therefore, to be taught to new members as

> the correct way to perceive, think, and feel about those problems.[7]

While thorough, this definition is rather complex and not easy to use day-to-day with your teams to help them assess and think about culture.

We have created a simple and instrumental definition of culture: culture is the collective *thinking* that creates the *states of mind* and *actions* that produce *results* in an organization.

While most of us pay attention to the obvious actions that show up in organizations, we tend to miss the hidden thought habits that are often unspoken, tacit, and influence these behaviors, ultimately generating our state of mind and results. As we pay more attention to those less obvious elements of thought habits and states of mind, the ability to change culture becomes more intuitive.

THE POWER OF CULTURE AT WORK: DERAILING A HALF-BILLION DOLLAR SYSTEM IMPLEMENTATION

It was just after the turn of the millennium. A large, global retail company committed to embarking on a four-year journey to implement a half-billion-dollar demand-chain system that would help it better manage inventory by using store-level data to pull product all the way through the system—from suppliers to the customer. The company hired a well-established and competent consulting firm to install and configure the system and even engaged a professor from a top business school who, quite literally, wrote the book on creating demand chains within large organizations.

A couple of years into the system configuration, most of the system settings were approved, the parameters were defined, the supply chain vendors had been plugged in, and the system was ready to go live. Although conventional wisdom would suggest that turning on a new supply or demand-chain system in retail organizations just before the holiday season would be ill-advised, the company ignored this wisdom due to its unhealthy state of mind. After years of long days, stress, and fatigue from the enormous undertaking, the company over-estimated its ability to successfully deploy the system.

Within the first few weeks, store leaders began to complain that they weren't seeing the volume of product they expected and needed to ramp up for the holidays. Waiting somewhat patiently, they continued to place calls to headquarters. Those calls quickly became a cacophony, with widespread clamoring for leaders to resolve the "issue" with the demand chain system and get the product out to the stores.

For those unfamiliar, the term "Black Friday" came to represent the approximate time in a retail organization when they "broke into the black" and finally started making a profit. In this company, the days around Black Friday typically produced as much revenue as entire weeks the rest of the year. With that in mind, you can imagine the fear and panic rapidly spreading across headquarters that the new system would not deliver the holiday product in a timely fashion and therefore cause the company to miss out on the prime period to sell.

A series of meetings ensued, led by merchants, where they gave very specific directions, stating it was imperative to "Get more product to the stores. Now. Period." The demand-chain consultants urged the team not to circumvent the system as it would render them unable to understand whether it was functioning properly and would destroy baseline readings of customer demand signals.

So, the merchants eventually decided that their teams would need to adjust the sensitivity in the dial settings such that smaller demand signals (which were purchased at the store level) generated a bigger pull of merchandise through the system —from the suppliers all the way through logistics to delivery to the local stores.

A few weeks passed and the stores expressed growing concern that the biggest sale days of the year were fast approaching, and they still didn't have the product they needed to satisfy their customers. That was it! The merchants had seen enough, and they instructed the demand planners to "crank up" to the maximum dial settings within each stage of the system.

The volume of products that arrived at malls across the United States within the next few weeks required hundreds of leased storage containers to store and a liquidation strategy to sell through the next quarter (with a multimillion dollar hit to the bottom line). Nevertheless, customers were happy to find nearly every variety of the product in stores for months.

What happened at this organization is not unusual, but it is a cautionary tale. We often install and configure systems, launch major strategic initiatives, acquire organizations, restructure our organizations, or launch new products and services without taking the fundamental step to notice and align our cultures to ensure that our people have what they need to achieve the desired outcome.

Ignoring culture does not mitigate its impact. Culture is continuously operating—influencing outcomes in both constructive and destructive ways, whether we notice it or not. In other words, we ignore culture at our peril.

THE ART AND SCIENCE OF CULTURE: AN ILLUMINATING FRAMEWORK

Every organization has an art and science to understand and transform the most important elements of culture, some obvious and some hidden. Let's explore this in depth.

Frameworks help you and your leadership team demystify the challenge of creating an organizational culture that works. Our framework takes the form of an iceberg that reflects both the *art* and *science* of culture—because, as we've said, the most powerful mechanisms at work in our culture are often *hidden* (Figure 2.1).

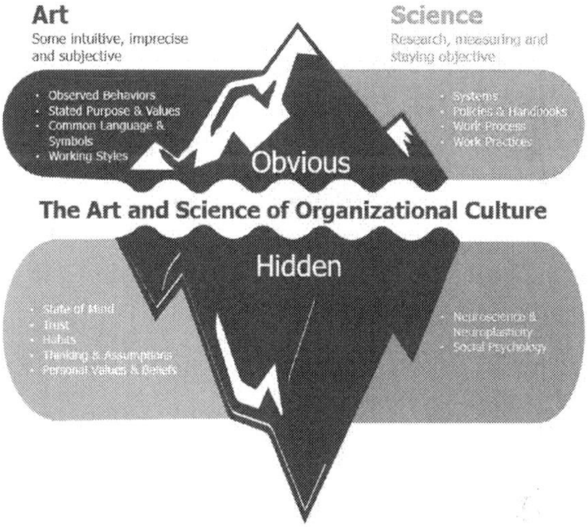

Figure 2.1 The art and science of organizational culture framework.

- In both the art and science of culture, there are obvious and hidden elements.
- The art includes the obvious subjective elements, such as shared purpose, stated values, and standard language and concepts.
- The art also includes hidden elements, such as thought habits, trust, states of mind, and personal beliefs.
- The science includes the *obvious* objective elements, such as handbooks, policies, systems, and procedures.
- The science also includes *hidden* elements such as neuroscience, which shows that culture is hard-wired

into our brains and other social sciences that predict human behavior.

A deeper understanding of cultural transformation includes observing how the elements or expressions of art and science in your culture are both obvious and hidden.

In the movie *A Few Good Men,* there is a court scene toward the end where a witness is asked to point out in the military guides where it explains how to issue a "Code Red," which was a disciplinary measure that had been eliminated from the military for safety reasons.[8] The defense was doing so to illustrate the fact that Code Reds were no longer condoned in the military.

The redirect from the prosecution was short and effective. The prosecutor (played by Tom Cruise) grabbed the same manual from the defense attorney's hands and presented it to the witness, and asked him to show the court where, in the manual, he was told where and when to eat. The witness paused and said, "Well, that isn't in there."

The prosecutor asked, "So, do you mean to tell us that you never had a meal at Guantanamo Bay?" The witness simply said, "Yes, sir. Three square meals a day, sir." Cruise finished, "Well, if you didn't learn it in the manual, then how did you know when and where to eat?" The witness answered, "I guess I just followed the guys at chow time, sir."

"No further questions," Cruise replied.

This simple exchange shows us that stated values (like Enron's of communication, respect, integrity, and excellence) are much less important predictors of behaviors than how people really do things within organizations.

Creating a clear purpose and shared values, updating policies and handbooks, and even creating employee value propositions are necessary to align your culture. However, they are insufficient to shape culture because the *hidden elements of culture are much more powerful than the obvious ones.*

The role of an effective leader is to balance the art and the science and to attend to the obvious and the hidden. A core process of principled transformation includes increasing the effectiveness of the obvious elements and the awareness of the hidden elements.

USING THE FRAMEWORK TO ILLUMINATE WHAT WAS ONCE HIDDEN

Let's return, briefly, to use these lenses to understand better the culture operating at the retailer who had a failed launch of a half-billion-dollar demand-chain system.

The CEO of the company was a merchant. He hired preeminent merchants from around the world to work with him. They tended to be promoted to CEOs of the brands in his organization. They had significant authority in the culture.

And yet, the operating norms of the demand-chain system required demand forecasters and planners to make decisions on inventory allocations. These decisions had traditionally been overseen (and often overruled) by the merchants.

Beginning with the obvious, though the planners were listed as decision makers in work practices, the art of the culture demanded merchants have decision rights (as they always had). They also were accustomed to using language that reflected their ability to make decisions and the planners' role in executing those decisions (with little influence).

The science of the culture included both new and old systems. Here, the new systems were developed to support the central role of the demand planners and forecasters, but the system was not yet adopted. Just weeks prior, they were using the old systems where their traditional thinking had merchants calling all the shots. The meetings, reports, and decision-making processes all reflected the old way of working and put the merchants in their known decision-making roles.

More hidden was the art of culture that included deeply held thought habits and beliefs (reflected in the role, authority, and even compensation) that merchants were dominant—essential, central, and effectively in charge. They made the decisions and weren't to be challenged. There was also a strong element of the state of mind that crept in; it was the holiday season, and leaders were "on the ropes" about beating sales plans. This led to leaders feeling tremendous anxiety and worry.

Finally, and perhaps most importantly, the brains of all parties who had been working for years in the old system had been hard-wired to operate in the old way. The employees had directly observed what had historically happened to those who publicly challenged the merchants and weren't about to repeat those *mistakes.*

After learning the lessons from the first launch of the system, with feedback, humility, and the shared experience of failure, the good news is that the teams were motivated to thoroughly explore the hidden elements of culture that were at play and began to shape them to take advantage of the new system. Imagine the benefit of seeing the culture clearly and intentionally influencing outcomes right from the start.

As you can see, the art and science, the obvious and hidden framework helps illuminate what is often genuinely misunderstood about how cultures operate within organizations. We all operate in a way that makes sense to each of us. What is less clear to others is why that is happening. The answer lies in the hidden art and science of organizational culture.

Clarifying your organizational purpose, your employee value proposition, your stated values, and your policies is critical. They are necessary but insufficient to cultivate the culture you really need to unlock the potential of your strategy.

You must also begin to notice and then intentionally shape the hidden elements of your organizational culture. As you become more aware of what's operating under the surface of what's obvious—those elements that are *hidden*—you will be able to shape and nurture them so they blossom, much like well-tended garden flowers and plants.

In addition to the client stories shared in this chapter, we have witnessed the following results when organizations became more aware and fluent in the hidden elements of their culture:

- Transitioned from nine years of declining top-line revenue to a growth year.
- Transitioned from two years of resisting agile in a 7,000-person IT organization to a growth mindset and rapid adoption.
- Transitioned from teams that were siloed and focused on their sub-brands to immense pride and collaboration in the parent organization, outperforming peers and the S&P by over 200 percent.
- Transitioned from a highly process-driven organization to one that balanced creativity and innovation with process, increasing value creation for customers, and driving up the stock price by over 500 percent in two years.

In the following chapters, we will explore how you can use this framework to shape your culture and create the immense value of doing so.

KEY TAKEAWAYS

- The essence of culture resides in the collective thinking and states of mind of organizational members.
- Many organizations focus on the obvious elements of culture yet ignore the hidden elements that are much more powerful.
- All major transformational initiatives require a corresponding change in culture.
- Transforming cultures by focusing on the hidden elements drives significant improvements to business results.

QUESTIONS TO CONSIDER

- What do the obvious elements, like stated purpose, values, onboarding, and employee policies, say about your organizational culture?
- What hidden forces might be creating what you experience in your culture? [Hint: It may be something that doesn't appear to make sense at face value. But understand that people do what makes sense to them.]
- How would operating with a beginner's mindset help you ask the right questions to uncover what is really at work in your organization's culture?

CHAPTER 3
MIRROR NEURONS AND NEUROPLASTICITY AT WORK

If you look the right way, you can see the whole world is a garden.

FRANCES HODGSON BURNETT

Cultures are like gardens: full of living things that can be intentionally shaped to produce a specific result (like producing vegetables or creating a calm and peaceful space to enjoy). Or, they can be left unattended and grow on their own to be much less efficient and productive. The leader's role is like a master gardener who directs others to generate the ideal culture that will unlock the organization's potential and unleash results.

Cultural norms and processes facilitate the dissemination of knowledge over generations and across geographies. Often, these are spread through social learning—by influencing and observing the interactions of other individuals.

Let's explore this idea through a story about a small group of monkeys. Imagine a researcher working with some monkeys in a large cage. In the center of the cage, hanging from the ceiling, is a large bunch of bananas. Under the bananas is a ladder. Soon, the first monkey begins to climb the ladder, and the researcher sprays cold water on that monkey *and all of the other monkeys.* Each time a monkey approaches the ladder, cold water is sprayed.

Very quickly, the monkeys (not wanting to be sprayed with cold water) start preventing the other monkeys from getting on the ladder. Then, over time, the researcher begins to replace the monkeys, one by one, with monkeys who were never sprayed by cold water but who noticed monkeys were always being prevented from accessing the ladder.

Finally, all the monkeys are replaced by other monkeys who were *never* sprayed with cold water, yet they continue the practice of preventing other monkeys from touching the ladder. Why? *Because that's the way we've always done it. It becomes a cultural norm.*

Based on an empirical study by Gordon Stephenson,[1] this story is powerful because it is easy to recognize similar adopted patterns of behavior in our workplaces. For example, we quickly learn whether a leader really wants to hear all voices in the room, at what level decisions are made, and whether risk-taking is a favored choice in an organization or is merely paid lip service. Applying the above story to our experiences in the workplace, we can understand why people in organizations tend to behave the way they do.

So, why do people act the way they do?

Surprisingly, culture transmission is quick—if done *right*. Throughout the hiring process, during your formal onboarding, and immediately after, you start to encounter the organization's group dynamics. If you are lucky, a trusted colleague will prepare you in advance for how to read the tea leaves, or the signals, in other words, how to behave in meetings or with certain leaders to achieve your goals.

If you are less lucky, you'll learn in the moment—either by observing others or by experiencing the effect of not being prepared directly—for "the way it works around here."

If you're the leader, know that the general behaviors around you are directly impacted by your *reflection of leadership.* That is, people tend to reflect back at you what you *model, reward,* or *tolerate.* We reference this concept of a leader's "reflection" to reinforce the role of mirror neurons in our brains.

LEVERAGING MIRROR NEURONS AND OUR LEADERSHIP REFLECTION

In the early 1990s, researchers in Italy found evidence of mirror neurons in lower primate species.[2] A mirror neuron is a neuron that fires when an animal observes another animal's behavior. In fact, our mirror neurons are constantly scanning the behaviors of those around us and they "mirror" the act of the other, as if the one observing was actually engaged in the behavior. Scientists have found evidence of these neurons in not only primates, but also humans.[3]

For example, if you watch a scary movie, you will experience physical reactions that can include sweaty palms, tense muscles, a drop in skin temperature, a spike in blood pressure, and an increased heart rate during certain scenes. Sometimes, you may even flinch at a moment when the character should be flinching. Another example is how yawns are contagious. When one person yawns, others nearby tend to do the same.

The potential implications of this discovery for our understanding of how cultures are formed and sustained are tremendous. For years we have recognized and observed the importance of culture around us, especially the social aspects.

But here, we see a biological and physiological basis for culture. Human beings are essentially *wired* for culture.

Consider that culture is the collective thinking that drives organizational behaviors and business results. And then further consider that collective thinking is a function of individual thinking. Individual thinking changes through individual learning. Individuals learn by experimentation (trying things and seeing what works) and by imitation (watching others and seeing what works).

Although the entire workings of mirror neurons are not precisely clear, some neuroscientists think these neurons may offer an understanding of the perception-action cycle. Nobel laureate Roger Sperry believed that perception leads to action and, in turn, that action leads to perception.[4] Sperry argued that this cycle was the fundamental logic of the nervous system and that this logic dictates how the brain transforms sensory input into behavior.

In fact, mirror neurons fire when we experience something as well as when we observe others experiencing the same thing. Thus, we now understand how we can rewire our brains as we socially learn from observing others—and this is where leaders as role models have such an impact in similar experiences.

MIRROR NEURONS ENTER THE WORKPLACE

Along with our genetic makeup and learned behaviors, mirror neurons explain much of the behavior we experience at work. For example, picture one of your colleagues bringing forward a new idea to improve the success of your organization—perhaps a new product, service, work practice, or automation. You watch your colleague present this new idea to the senior team at your organization and see how they respond. While you observe this interaction, you may experience some of the same feelings that your colleague is directly experiencing. You are also learning how to behave in a similar situation in the future.

At one large global bank, the CEO launched a major initiative on innovation and growth to help digitally transform the outdated organization and propel the business forward. As part of this initiative, the bank began recruiting heavily on the West Coast for creative and innovative talent with strong digital capabilities.

Shortly after this new talent arrived, they brought forward the new ideas necessary to advance the business and observed each other, one by one, having those ideas shot down by upper management. After the senior team went through this culture experience, they started to notice how their tendency to shoot down ideas actually stifled innovation and led to increased turnover with the talent they so desperately needed.

If you don't take the time to notice this tendency, it stays in your subconscious and just becomes "how we do things around here." Once we do notice, we can take action to change it.

YOUR LEADERSHIP TEAM IS NOT FOCUSING ON BUSINESS IMPACT

We were engaged by the CIO of a large global consumer company to help enable an agile transformation in the IT function. As we worked through this process, the CIO reiterated how important it was for his organization to be focused on *outcomes* and not just *output*. By this, he meant that he wanted to be sure that what his team implemented positively impacted the business (outcome) instead of just completing projects (output).

When we prepared a scorecard to measure the success of the culture transformation, we reviewed the CIO's existing metrics. The key measures for his more than 500 employees included the strong business outcome of running projects *on time* and *on budget*.

How long do you think it took the employees to culturally transmit that, while the CIO said outcomes were more important, performance reviews and financial incentives were tied to *on time* and *on budget?* [Hint: usually, after just one performance review cycle, *everyone* in an organization knows what really matters to a leader.]

IS YOUR EXECUTIVE TEAM FOCUSING ON THEIR OWN DIVISIONS OR FUNCTIONS AND NOT THE ORGANIZATION'S GREATER GOOD?

In another example, we interviewed a CEO as we prepared for a culture transformation workshop with his team. Repeatedly, he told us that he wanted his team to step up and lead more of the corporate strategic initiatives. The CEO said he felt like his team was focused on their own function or division, not on the corporation's greater good.

As we conducted the workshop, we raised the issue (after generating some positive energy in the team). The CEO asked why people weren't more willing to lead the corporate initiatives. Quickly, an outspoken team member said, "What, so you can make it the way you want it anyway?"

The team members all agreed that the CEO had a tendency to "always want to put his stamp" on things. In fact, he tended to want things done his way and his team members quickly learned that the energy they put into leading corporate initiatives would often go to waste because the CEO largely reworked their carefully prepared recommendations. And in the process, he demotivated his team.

In a subsequent session with this team, we also learned that the overwhelming majority of an executive team member's compensation was tied to division or department goals, not corporate ones. The correlation is nearly perfect in our experiences studying executive behaviors and compensation. While there is always an intention to do what is good for the team, most of us tend to do what we are rewarded to do—what we are paid to deliver. It's Steve Kerr's classic observation of the folly of rewarding A while hoping for B, in which reward systems undermine the stated goal.[5]

Once you do a little detective work, it's pretty easy to see why people choose to behave the way they do. Chances are they tend to do whatever offers the best and most *personal* of rewards beyond compensation.

DEVELOPING A FEEDBACK-RICH CULTURE

The reflection of your leadership also works in very positive ways. We once worked with a CEO who had one of the most feedback-rich cultures we've ever seen. In one of our earliest 1:1 interactions with her, she asked us for feedback. Surprised, we quickly recalled what we had seen her do that morning and fumbled through some advice.

The next time we saw her, she asked for additional feedback. This time, we came more prepared with some positive and constructive feedback. And we also asked for feedback from her. And she too, was ready to deliver a thoughtful and robust set of suggestions.

This mutually well-prepared, frank dialogue session played out in conversation after conversation we had with this leader and company. Even more beneficially, our sessions led to a dynamic of candid feedback becoming a cultural norm—just being "how we do things around here."

Understanding your reflection of leadership is one *hidden* element that is critical to transforming your culture. Why do we call this a "reflection of leadership?" Because we tend to see actions in our organization that reflect what we model, reward, and tolerate. These actions in others are the culture at work and reflect our leadership—propagated by mirror neurons at work in our brains.

NEUROPLASTICITY: THE BRAIN THAT CHANGES ITSELF

In his book *The Brain That Changes Itself,* Norman Doidge describes the brain's ability to rewire itself. This rewiring is called neuroplasticity, which shows how our brains can physically change their structure over time. It has been said that neurons that *fire together, wire together.* As we have learned from the previous examples, these mirror neurons are constantly firing. This results in them continuously forming new connections.[6]

This rewiring is happening, whether we notice it or not. In fact, the vast majority of this rewiring happens subconsciously. This is essentially how we create habits at work. Some of these habits serve us well, but some can work against us as we pursue the business's strategy. This latter group is where you should pay attention and commit resources to additional rewiring. Thus, attuning your brain through neuroplasticity is *the key* building block of culture transformation.

BE OPEN TO DRIVE MORE RAPID LEARNING AND INNOVATION IN YOUR ORGANIZATION

One of the major purposes of your organization is to produce organizational learning that drives organizational change and generates business results.

However, through our extensive observations over the years, we have found that what is needed in the modern business environment is a more effective way to think. Why? Your thinking defines your way of *being*. The challenge in today's business environment is to escape or evolve beyond our habitual patterns of individual and collective thinking or culture and then develop a more effective way of thinking. If you are to overcome new challenges, you need a new way of thinking and, even more so, a new way of being.

Consider the daunting factors that contribute to the complexity of organizational life:

- Speed of the world
- Global scale
- Complex problems
- Growing distrust of institutions

Speed of the world includes such factors as rapid and constant changes in technology, the speed of information dissemination, constant changes in the workplace, relentless social media exposure, and the spread of pandemics enabled by modern travel.

Many of the same factors impacting the world's speed impact companies on a global scale. Technology, information dissemination, social media, and pandemics all have a global reach. In addition, the global economy is more interconnected than ever, with national economies impacting one another down to the local level.

The speed of the world paired with global scale has contributed to the rise of numerous complex problems, including mental health issues, obesity, drug addiction, chronic disease states, environmental concerns, social justice issues, and cybercrime, to name just a few. These complex problems are experienced and impact all levels of society in all parts of the world.

Finally, we have also witnessed a rise in mistrust of traditional institutions, including governments and political systems, religions, legal systems, education systems, and healthcare systems, as these institutions have struggled to deal with complex economic, social, and political challenges. In fact, the 2021 Edelman Trust Barometer shows that CEO credibility is at an all-time low in many countries and that 56 percent of respondents say that business leaders are purposely trying to mislead people by saying things they know are false or gross exaggerations.[7]

These challenges speak to the need for new thinking, rapid learning, and resilience at the individual and team level and for businesses, most importantly, at the organization levels. The capacity to sustain learning and resilience is fundamentally the ability to leverage neuroplasticity—in other words, the ability of our brains and nervous systems to adapt to continuous change.

KEY TAKEAWAYS

- Dysfunctional behaviors are *learned at work* through social learning and reinforcement, as are healthy behaviors like experimentation, curiosity, and collaboration.
- Mirror neurons in our brains constantly pay attention to the behaviors and consequences around us within an organization.
- As we learn, our brains embed these behaviors into our normal ways of working through neuroplasticity.
- Culture transmission (how we do things around here) can be quick—if done right.

QUESTIONS TO CONSIDER

- What would be the value of taking a step back and assessing "the way we do things around here?"
- What dysfunctional behaviors in your organization are barriers to business performance?
- Why might it make sense for people to behave in ways that impede your results? (What behaviors or consequences might they have seen in the past?)
- How might some of your actions influence the culture around you?

CHAPTER 4
IS YOUR CULTURE ACTUALLY OKAY?

One fish asks another, "How's the water?"
The other fish replies, "What the hell is water?"

DAVID FOSTER WALLACE

In a sense, culture is like water we swim in. If we are constantly in the culture, it becomes our normal, and we tend not to notice it. For example, have you ever joined a new company and noticed so many details about how people act? Why do they start meetings late and run long? Or why do they always start right on time? Why do people tend to speak up in meetings? Or why do they always sit quietly and wait for the leader to speak?

As you begin to ask good questions of your new colleagues, you start to see that those who have worked in the organization for an extended time act the way they do because "that's the way we do things here." That's the water they swim in. In other words, they no longer notice how they act or how their teammates act.

HOW CAN YOU RAISE AWARENESS OF YOUR CULTURE?

To begin to notice what's working well and what isn't in an organization's culture, we often help clients through a simple exercise to raise awareness. We ask senior teams to write down a brief list of the behaviors common to the highest performing team they have ever been a part of. This could include sports teams, music groups, military experience, volunteer organizations, family outings, or teams within organizations.

After writing down their responses one by one, the senior team members read their lists for the rest of the team to hear. With one group of only 12 senior team members, we ended up with a set of nearly 70 distinct behaviors that were *most important,* in their collective eyes, to building a successful team. At the end of this successful exercise, the CEO exclaimed, "I believe that all of these behaviors are critical for success, but now how can we possibly get down to just three to five to guide our culture?"

Herein lies the fundamental problem facing most leadership teams: a lack of alignment around a critical set of strategic behaviors that will unleash the company's strategy. Seeing a senior team value 70 different behaviors will not only confuse an organization, but also lead to deeper dysfunction as each leadership team member will believe *their* way is the *right* way.

The solution? To align your culture, it's critical to get to a small set of values (often with defined behaviors) that are most important to execute 100 percent of the time (rather than dozens of behaviors that are demonstrated some of the time).

The other reason we do this activity is to improve the self-awareness of each leader. After we align on a final set of three to five organizational values, we ask the leaders to go back and compare their original lists of critical behaviors with the list of values. We ask leaders to consider:

- Which ones were contained within their lists?
- Which ones were missing and why?
    - Did they forget?
    - Are they blind spots? Or are they development opportunities?
- Which ones would drive the best business results?

If your senior team prioritizes different behaviors for their teams, is it any wonder that you don't have a clear handle on what the current culture is in the organization and what the ideal culture should be? Having an aligned senior team with a clear understanding of the current and ideal culture is the most important first step. So how do you take that step?

HOW TO DIAGNOSE YOUR CULTURE IN A WEEK

There is no shortage of diagnostic surveys that can help you diagnose your culture. There are also many capable firms who can help you conduct focus groups and carefully compile themes into a report that helps you better understand your current culture.

This is an essential first step, but what we have found is that there are a few challenges with the typical approaches to diagnosing culture:

- They take too long (and cost too much).
- They don't include both quantitative and qualitative findings.
- They are using outdated frameworks that were appropriate for the traditional organizations from the 1980s.

Quite simply, if your diagnostic process is going to take three to six months, you will likely end up with an outdated view of your culture, and no progress on advancing your culture will have been made. Or worse, in one of the major firms that conduct engagement and climate surveys, you may learn that your scores will *go down* after 12 months from where they started before engaging with you.

We also continue to see culture diagnostics disconnected from business results—showing marked progress on their cultural dimensions while business outcomes continue to slip. Why?

Ideally, you can leverage technology to assess your culture in weeks, not months. For example, in one organization, we were asked to assess its culture and report back within a week. We conducted our proprietary diagnostic survey and AI-based digital focus groups and shared the culture profile the following week.

The important considerations are to have a process that is:

- Modern, reflecting current factors
- Valid and reliable
- Efficient, leveraging technology and AI
- Tied to business outcomes
- Conducted confidentially by an independent third party

Keep in mind that fees and timing are proportional for culture transformations. By this, we mean an assessment should take about 10 percent of the time and budget for your culture transformation. So, when firms come in and suggest that it will take hundreds of thousands of dollars and three to six months to give you an assessment of their current state, consider a second opinion. (And, just think: they will be measuring *your* agility!)

THE MOST IMPORTANT CURRENT FACTORS THAT PREDICT HIGH-PERFORMING CULTURES

If culture is such a strong predictor of organizations' operating and economic performance, which elements of culture are the most critical to develop? To answer this question, we draw upon decades of research and our collective years of experience working with CEOs and leading culture transformations. Many firms' models of culture tie back to the competing values framework (CVF) that was created in 1983 by Robert Quinn and John Rohrbaugh.[1]

The CVF framework defines four archetypes of organizations:

- Adhocracy (a flexible, informal structure)
- Market-oriented
- Hierarchy
- Family

Though firms have modified the language a bit, many still work from a model developed for how firms operated back in the 1980s. We have used and found the CVF framework to be helpful in some regards and yet insufficiently detailed or modern enough to use to systematically shape cultures.

We believe it's time for something new. Based on a meta-analysis of culture frameworks and our own experiences, we have developed a modern model that helps organizations build cultures the way they naturally evolve in the workplace. This modern model begins by focusing on the health of individual leaders. It then describes how these leaders effectively work in teams and how aligned teams support the broad organizational ambition.

We created the Culture Capability Assessment™ (Figure 4.1) to help companies rapidly measure their capabilities to develop their culture systematically. This model covers the most common cultural challenges facing organizations. These challenges were derived from speaking to hundreds of leaders in recent years. In particular, CEOs currently express a greater need for:

- Collaborating
- Having more accountability
- Focusing on the greater good
- Developing more agility and resilience
- Being inclusive

Often, organizations spend time on the evident and noisy things in their culture. For instance, in surveys and focus groups, they may find that employees want better work/life balance, more benefits, more variety in cafeteria meal options, to bring their dog to work, to have bean bag chairs and standing desks, or to be able to reorganize or change their pay for the umpteenth time. And yet, the culture noise can sometimes drown out the signal that we are trying to pick up in effective culture diagnostics.

All of these are interesting but unreliable ways to transform and intentionally shape your culture to drive performance. And, paying too much attention to the obvious and noisy aspects of culture will cause you to miss the subtle, more hidden elements (like the collective thinking and states of mind in the organization, as discussed earlier). These elements can quickly align and unleash your culture.

Organizations often move through successive reorganizations and redesign compensation systems repeatedly to try and drive the behaviors they want to see. Yet while doing this, they completely neglect to explore and shift the underlying thought habits that create the organization's undesirable behaviors.

Once you understand why it makes sense to someone to behave that way—maybe they see their boss do it, they get praise for doing it, they've always done it that way, they see their peers doing it (and getting ahead), and so on—you can more reliably shift their thinking and, ultimately, their actions.

SUCCESS BEGINS WITH A STATE OF MIND

One often overlooked source of lower-performing behaviors is employees' *state of mind.* When people are worried, stressed, anxious, or feeling insecure, they are probably not going to perform at a high level. They won't tend to take risks, give each other helpful feedback, or be very inclusive.

Like a circuit breaker, our brains can trigger an amygdala trip that causes us to freeze, fight, or take flight. Leaders can also accidentally trigger an unhealthy state of mind by something they do or say (as we discussed in Chapter 1). Suffice it to say, when your employees are in a freeze, fight, or flight mode, they will be unable to choose the ideal ways to act in your organization.

Shifting a team member's state of mind to be more positive, optimistic, and confident will naturally generate more healthy behaviors. So, when we shape cultures, we start first with an individual's state of mind.

CULTURES ARE SHAPED FIRST AT AN *INDIVIDUAL LEVEL*

Since organizational culture primarily resides in each employee's mind, cultures must be shaped one person at a time. Change happens by rewiring our brains. The bottom line? All *cultural change* is *biological change*. We create culture by who we are, how we work, and our level of integrity.

Business challenges turn around due to a healthier state of mind

In 2011, ABC High-Tech Manufacturing had a big problem. As a result of the worldwide debt crisis of 2008 and 2009, both of its major markets imploded. In one market, product pricing had dropped from 50 percent above manufacturing costs to 50 percent below in just over 30 days. In other words, the company was losing money on every unit produced. In the other markets, worldwide demand was down due to factory closures.

The competition was fierce. Every quarter brought more demands for lower prices and higher quality. In addition, the company had just acquired several firms and had yet to develop a unified culture. The culture amounted to a patchwork of various purposes and values across the globe with no sense of there being one team all working together. This made collaboration and accountability very difficult to establish and internal competition the norm. Further, after the stock price dropped from $15 per share to $1.50 per share, morale in the organization was at an all-time low.

The executive team knew that drastic action was needed, although the exact path was unclear. What *was* clear was the need for dramatic changes in strategy and structure. However, the organization's health or, more precisely, the *lack of health* made large change efforts nearly impossible.

During a critical session we held, the CEO and leadership team made a fundamental decision. They decided to lead with culture to increase the organization's health so that it would endure the magnitude of change needed and not merely implode under the weight of change. The decision made was an outcome of the realization that:

- The organization's milieu directly reflected how the leadership team was currently leading.
- The leadership team made a conscious choice to do something new and different.
- They mustered up the discipline through their sense of *collective IMpowerment* (a term we use to describe personal accountability—leveraging the power within) to go out and make this happen.

As the leadership team diagnosed the current state and defined the needed future state, the team became aware that the *CEO and leadership team* would have to own, live, and lead the change effort. In other words, the team understood that if they expected the organization to be more collaborative, innovative, and accountable, they would have to become that change to have the authority to guide the change. And the CEO knew that he would need to lead the way and, as such, was the driving force behind the turnaround.

While *walking the walk* is cliché, it is critical that we *do* what we *say*. Living the culture you want is the challenge, the mountain that will always need to be climbed by your leadership team.

If CEOs need and want new behaviors, from collaboration to inclusivity, where do they start? They must begin with themselves. This is a new imperative for leaders. They must look at how their own beliefs, habits, and thinking led to *creating the current culture* and explore ways they want to be more personally aligned with the ideal culture. From there, intact teams develop team behaviors that are aligned with the ideal culture. It is only through impacting multiple teams that we can reliably shape cultures at the organizational level to produce the outcomes identified in the business strategy.

To measure and improve at each of these levels, we use our Culture Capability Assessment™ to measure *leader fitness, team alignment,* and *organizational health* (see Figure 4.1). Let's explore the model in a bit more detail.

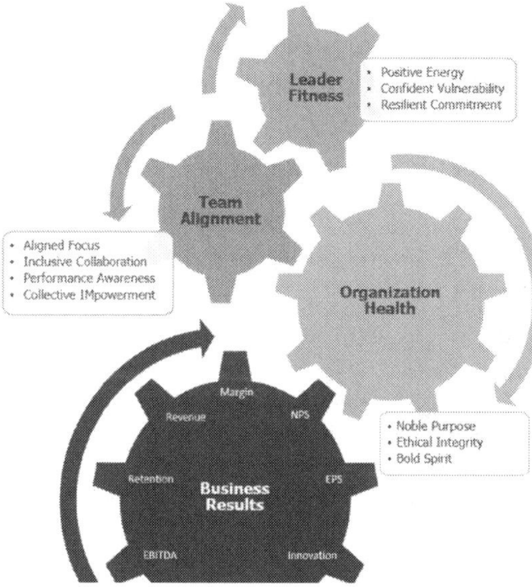

Figure 4.1 Our Culture Capability Assessment™ framework.

LEADER FITNESS

What we know from seeing leader fitness at work in the organization after the organization is that culture is a *reflection of leadership.* What we mean by this is that the behaviors of employees tend to reflect those of leaders in the organization. As we learned in the last chapter, employees constantly use *mirror neurons* in their brains that are continuously scanning for *how things are done around here,* so they can continue to adapt. The leader's reflection is the most dominant in modeling behaviors for the organization to mimic.

So, what do effective leaders need to have to develop high-performing cultures? We found three dimensions of leader fitness to be critical:

- **Positive energy** measures a leader's ability to be optimistic, operate with the best intentions, and generate positive energy for themselves and others.
- **Confident vulnerability** measures a leader's willingness to take risks, share mistakes and learn and grow confidently. (We'll discuss this in more depth in Chapter 10.)
- **Resilient commitment** measures a leader's ability to grow from setbacks, quickly respond to change, and engage their teams.

Positive energy is contagious and necessary to engage the organization. It creates a positive spirit in others and motivates them to want to join you in the culture journey. Perhaps the most important in this set is *confident vulnerability.* What we have learned about leading culture transformation (or most any change) within large organizations is the importance of a *balance* of confidence and vulnerability.

The norm for most businesses has been confidence without vulnerability. And yet, vulnerability is critical to building trust and elevating performance.[2] Imagine trying to get thousands of employees to follow you through change without trust. It doesn't work.

When CEOs ask us to "fix their teams or their dysfunctional organizations" without being open to small shifts themselves, we have to be honest with them: we can't. However, when leaders demonstrate the willingness to accept that they may not be perfect and that they can learn and grow, then we have a wonderful starting place for culture transformation—a leader with a *growth mindset.*[3]

Resilient commitment describes the ability to continue to pursue a goal. Even when faced with setbacks or failures, leaders persevere and continue to press ahead, as in this example:

- A biotech and science firm lost critical patents in the late 1980s.
- They were spun off and bought by a foreign firm.
- Private equity came in and eviscerated the place.
- They went public and the value exploded.
- The Chinese opened up a new plant and doubled the amount of material available in the market, causing prices (and the company's value) to plummet.
- They spun off again and were bought by another foreign firm. As a result, they are now more successful than ever.

TEAM ALIGNMENT

Only when you have consistent fitness or a healthy state of mind of individual leaders can you enhance their ability to work as one aligned team. In our experience, if leaders are unhealthy in their thinking, trying to get them aligned is a fruitless activity. When leaders are in a healthy state of mind, they can have authentic conversations that lead to alignment. And team alignment is what CEOs and employees want from senior teams. By team alignment, we mean a team operating with:

- **Aligned focus:** operating from a clear and consistent set of priorities—when the team is together and when they are apart.
- **Inclusive collaboration:** operating from a level of trust, valuing healthy differences, and considering all perspectives when making decisions. They promote a sense of belonging and make decisions for the greater good of the organization.
- **Performance awareness:** bringing forward the critical role of seeking feedback, sharing feedback, and providing one-on-one feedback in the moment to help one another continue to grow and learn.

- **Collective IMpowerment**: having a bias for action, leveraging high initiative and freedom to do a job, and clearly seeing your role in contributing to its outcome.

COLLECTIVE IMPOWERMENT WILL TRANSFORM YOUR ORGANIZATION

> The question isn't who is going to let me, it's who will stop me.
>
> AYN RAND

Yes, *collective IMpowerment* is a play on words. And that's for a reason. Low levels of accountability plague our organizations and yet, we all feel we are willing to "hold our teams accountable" or "empower them to lead." What we find is that this sort of thinking gets teams and organizations stuck because often the term "accountable" is used in the third person. In fact, using the third person is a slippery slope that allows people to focus mostly on what *others* failed to do instead of looking at what more *they* can do.

While we often hear that leaders expect employees to be accountable or empowered, what ultimately decides behaviors is the thinking of the individual. Accountability or empowerment isn't something that can be demanded. If an individual is operating from a lower *state of mind*, like fear, or they have been socially taught that they should keep their head down, or not to make mistakes, then they will behave accordingly.

What we help foster in organizations is *IM*powerment. IMpowerment is a deliberate play on the word "empowerment." Here, we intentionally use the *first person* and focus. IMpowerment contains the prefix "IM," which means *from within*. When we help leaders and teams see the power within each of them, they cannot help but notice their role in their lives, their teams, and the world.

As one of our favorite clients would say: "You either happen to the world or the world happens to you." IMpowerment is how we describe "happening to the world."

We were working with a large consumer company that had been working on a culture of accountability for nearly a decade. Yet when we did the diagnostic, we found that the organization reported lower levels of responsibility that were still a problem. Then, as we worked with the leadership team, we heard clearly that the leader would hold this team accountable for change. Then this team said they would, in turn, keep their teams accountable, and so on.

In this case, it is important to notice that they were operating in the third person—holding others accountable—rather than looking for their personal role in an outcome. That puts the focus and attention on what *someone else* did or didn't do. When everyone in an organization is focused on what someone else is doing, we find very low levels of *personal ownership*—what we call IMpowerment.

THE PROBLEM WITH ACCOUNTABILITY

If you ask any human being, "Are you accountable for your actions?" it often puts them on the defensive. Being accountable is a loaded term that often triggers the amygdala, sending us into a fearful fight or flight mode. As a result, we feel the need to defend ourselves against the potential consequences of appearing unaccountable.

Contrast this question with a better one, such as, "How could you have an even greater impact on a positive outcome in a relationship or project?" Here they can easily tell you what else they may try. This type of question amplifies IMpowerment in employees.

The key to understanding *collective IMpowerment* can be described by the experience of a client with whom we had been working for about a year. When reconnecting with the senior team, they had just learned before the beginning of the meeting that one of their rising stars had departed to join a competitor. We expected to hear that they really weren't that good anyway, that the rising star was making a mistake, or that they had done all they could to retain her. And yet, here's what we heard:

- Direct supervisor: "I should have stayed closer to her and the hiring manager for the other job she wanted internally. And acknowledged the impact that not being selected had on her."
- Chief human resources officer: "Well, actually, I'm responsible for succession, and I should have had more conversations with her to make sure she knew that she was critical to our future success and that we had her in a few spots in the succession plan."
- Chief executive officer: "Hold on a minute, I'm probably the one who fed her ego a bit too much. I wanted her to know how valuable she was, but I wasn't clear enough on how many years it may take her to get to the next level. I gave her unrealistic expectations."

This conversation is a powerful lesson in *collective IMpowerment*. These leaders all recognized the power they had to influence the outcome, and the discussion was all in the first person versus the third person. That is often a disguise for having lower levels of accountability at that moment. For example, saying: "I'll hold Mary accountable for this" is often a subtle way of blaming others and failing to acknowledge the power you had to influence the outcome directly.

IMpowerment is first-person accountability, and collective IMpowerment is an even more powerful way to maximize your collective influence to generate the best outcomes in any interaction you share. It has the added benefit of reducing the negative stress and toxicity of finger-pointing, blame, and worse, undermining people when they make mistakes or don't meet expectations. As one executive we know said, "When we hire them, they're great. So, how do they become a-holes?"

ORGANIZATIONAL HEALTH

Once you have fit leaders who are aligned as a team, you can more rapidly and efficiently create true organizational health, which is characterized by the three principles below. Want IMpowerment? Then you need to focus on enabling your organization's:

- **Noble purpose:** The way your organization focuses on the customer and the positive impact you make on the world.
- **Ethical integrity:** The foundation on which your entire organization operates, including doing the right thing and acting in the best interests of your employees.
- **Bold spirit:** Your organization's willingness to try new things, expect high performance, focus on quality, and anticipate change.

Noble purpose

Since the 1970s, we've known that work is about "a search . . . for daily meaning as well as daily bread."[4] In fact, in a recent study of 2,285 American professionals across 26 industries, Achor et. al found that nine out of 10 people are willing to earn less money to do more meaningful work. And, when people are doing more meaningful work, they are more productive, generating nearly $10,000 per employee, per year.[5]

Organizations with a strong and shared sense of purpose are clear about the greater good they create and articulate it:

- Southwest Airlines: Connect people to what's important in their lives through friendly, reliable, and low-cost air travel.
- CVS Health: Helping people on their path to better health.
- Google: To organize the world's information and make it universally accessible and useful.
- Walmart: Saving people money so they can live better.
- Tesla: To accelerate the world's transition to sustainable energy.
- Harley-Davidson: Fulfilling dreams of personal freedom.

Who wouldn't want to be a part of creating such positive change in the world? And yet, many organizations still focus on creating shareholder value, which is, of course, important, but no longer enough. Shareholder value simply does not inspire, attract, or retain the best talent.

In fact, in 2019, nearly 200 CEOs (including those at Apple, Walmart, and others) as part of the Business Roundtable issued a statement expanding the purpose of a corporation to include not only shareholders, but also employees, suppliers, and the environment.[6]

Ethical Integrity

The foundation for organizational culture that enables your ability to align, collaborate, innovate, and perform is *trust*. And, trust stems from doing the right things, being authentic, and being vulnerable. There are two elements to consider when evaluating trust in organizations: *ethics* describes external factors and *integrity* is reflected in our internal choices for how we act.

Ethics are often dictated by your organization in a set of values, code of conduct, or code of ethics. These guides describe how to behave in a manner that reflects what your organization believes is the *right* thing to do, especially in situations that are typically encountered and may present dilemmas. In one large accounting firm, the CEO would always say, "Let's always be on the right side of right." We can then use these guides to evaluate our decisions and actions.

In one large retail organization, the CHRO was bringing forward a new parental leave policy, which would dramatically increase the cost of labor, to allow new parents time at home with their growing families. Because she felt the cost would be significant to the company, she presented the executive team with a more conservative recommendation. While she was presenting, another executive asked her how this proposal was aligned with their value to "do the right thing." She paused and said, actually I think we should offer a much richer parental leave package, but I was concerned about the expense. The executive team agreed and went forward with the decision to provide one of the most generous parental leave policies in their industry.

Integrity comes from within. It shows up in how we act—typically whether we are honest and fair. We also can observe this in cultures as a ratio of what we *say* to what we *do* (the say/do ratio). When we say we want to be innovative, but act in a way that limits creativity and punishes risk-taking, we are not in integrity. In fact, when our say/do ratio is out of balance, we breed cynicism. People begin to disassociate what we say from what will actually happen. For example, when we say that it is important to reward employees for both their results and how they got results, but we pay people based only on the numbers, there is a disconnect between what we say and what we do.

When what we say and do are disconnected, it is a function of what is obvious and what is hidden. The *obvious* element here is the stated code of conduct; the *hidden* element comes from our internal thinking being out of alignment with what is stated in the code. In the case above, we may think that results are most important and how we lead is less important. Therefore, we reward results over how we lead and work with others. For us, integrity is a function of aligning the obvious and hidden elements of culture.

Bold spirit

While ethical integrity is straightforward, we want to take a moment to explore what we mean by establishing a *bold spirit* in organizations. Too often, we encounter organizations that are constrained by the past. We hear statements from leaders such as:

- This is what we've always produced.
- This is how we've always produced it,
- We want to do a few percent better than last year.

It is increasingly important for organizations to build a bold spirit in an age of disruption because it is necessary to challenge the status quo. And, with continuous disruption it's also imperative to be open to new possibilities. This includes being agile in the marketplace, trying new things, encouraging risk-taking, and placing bets on where the future will reward the organization.

As we have used the Culture Capability Assessment™ framework, we have found that it is intuitive in diagnosing the current state and provides a clear road map of how to advance your culture, step-by-step. First, focus on leader fitness and, once leaders are ready, explore how to fully align and develop high-performing teams as building blocks of the organization. Finally, focus on the organization-level drivers that will help you align your business strategy and fully unlock your potential.

Most importantly, move quickly through the diagnostic to get to your ideal culture definition and bring it to life—through your leaders, teams, and organization.

KEY TAKEAWAYS

- Culture becomes hidden—like the water we swim in—if we don't pause to notice it.
- An inspiring organizational purpose can increase engagement and productivity by offering employees meaningful work.
- Three critical factors predict healthy and high-performing cultures: leader fitness, team alignment, and organization health.
- Collective IMpowerment is a measure of a team's ability to generate power from within and an important predictor of firm performance.
- The Culture Capability Assessment™ is a framework not only for diagnosis, but also for how to shape culture through leaders, teams, and then the organization.

QUESTIONS TO CONSIDER

- Which of the elements within the Culture Capability Assessment™ are likely strengths for you and your senior team?
- Positive energy
- Confident vulnerability
- Resilient commitment
- Aligned focus
- Inclusive collaboration
- Performance awareness
- Collective IMpowerment
- Noble purpose
- Ethical integrity
- Bold spirit
- Which elements might be lacking as you look deeper into your organization?

- What economic value would likely be created for your firm by improving in one or more of these areas?

CHAPTER 5

HOW DO YOU BUILD CULTURE CAPABILITY?

> *Greatness is not a function of circumstance. Greatness, it turns out, is largely a matter of conscious choice, and discipline.*
>
> **JIM COLLINS, *GOOD TO GREAT***

There are only so many strategic choices you can make as an organization. By strategic, we mean what organizations choose to do (and not do) to compete in the markets. The overwhelming majority of strategies we see include:

- Developing new, innovative products
- Cross-selling more products to existing clients
- Improving the customer experience
- Entering early into a new market
- Becoming a low-cost provider
- Developing a differentiated product
- Improving customer retention
- Merging or acquiring a complementary firm
- Vertically integrating to control more of the value chain

- Adjusting price to balance margin with revenue
- Developing a platform or ecosystem for markets

What you may notice about each of these choices is there is often little that can be done to *sustain* your advantage after making any choice. Move quickly into a new market and you can turn around and see a dozen others quickly following. Develop new, innovative products and watch your competition do the same. Any adjustments you make in pricing will quickly be balanced by competitors in the markets.

This is not to say that strategy is not important; it is very important to make the right decisions. But in a volatile, uncertain, complex, and ambiguous (VUCA) world,[1] even the best strategic decisions don't remain the best decisions for long.

The frequent need to adapt your strategy to compete in markets creates a lack of alignment between strategy, structure, culture, and high-performance work practices (as discussed in Chapter 2). Even if you had the greatest internal culture champion or the resources to bring in a consultant to diagnose your culture, moving through a transformation process and get the organization "locked in" to a new way of behaving that aligns with the strategy, your strategy will eventually change. And, as a result, helping the culture adjust to the new strategy will be important to maintain strategic alignment.

CONTINUOUSLY ALIGNING CULTURE TO STRATEGY

The most important capability that we help organizations develop is a *culture capability*. By this, we mean that we help organizations develop an agile culture *that can transform itself* to unlock the strategy you choose as quickly as possible. This capability will help you continuously adapt to external markets and unlock the power of your strategy, as it evolves.

As you consider your current culture capability, consider the Culture Capability Maturity Model (Figure 5.1), which illustrates the differences we see between the most and least mature culture capabilities within organizations we have served. The levels are not good or bad—they just are. Noticing where you sit within the maturity model will help you identify actions you can take to ensure that you are leveraging your culture effectively to enable your business.

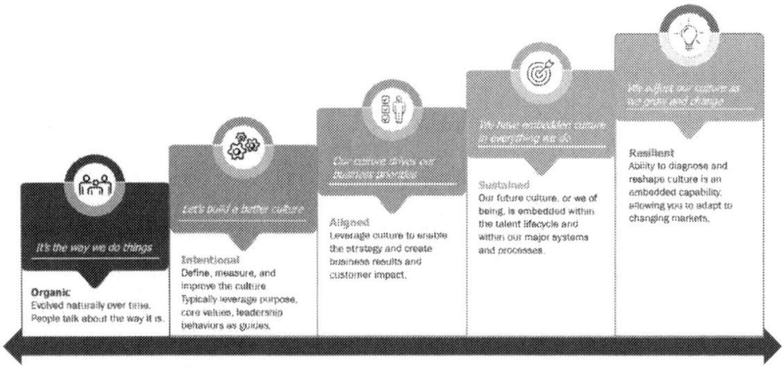

Figure 5.1 The Culture Capability Maturity Model.

Organic

Fundamentally, the most basic level of culture capability is what we call *organic*. This means that the culture has been allowed to evolve on its own. We often find this in startups and even in relatively mature, founder-led organizations. In many cases, we hear that if we have to write it down, there is something wrong with how we lead the organization. Yet some of these organizations have become as large as tens of thousands of employees with turnover rates as high as 60 percent per year.

This level of culture capability is only appropriate for a small subset of relatively stable organizations with a sustainable competitive advantage. They must also have a tremendous amount of interaction between employees to keep the undocumented culture alive. After these organizations evolve to be larger and more complex, they will quickly find that culture is now a causal factor of their business success and not just a byproduct of how things get done.

Intentional

The next level of culture capability is *intentional*. At this level, organizations tend to define the culture they want, invest the time and energy to create it, and measure themselves against the defined culture. Often, we will see organizations that want to be a *best place to work*, have *high engagement scores*, have a *safety culture*, or some other fundamentally important element of operating a business.

It's an important step to move from organic to intentional because the intentional level provides you with a plan for what you want the culture to be and how you are performing against that plan. At this stage, human resources typically define and measure the culture and report to other executives, the board, and the broader organization. This is a fundamentally important level as there is a growing awareness of the power of choosing your ideal culture and measuring progress.

Aligned

The next level of culture capability is focused on *aligning* the culture with the business strategy to enhance business performance. At this level, engagement or a great work environment isn't just about engagement. In partnership with CHROs, savvy leaders are fluent in their businesses and seek to align their culture to enable people in the organization to execute the business strategy. They realize that, as business strategies shift, cultural shifts need to quickly follow to maintain strategic alignment.

For example, in a large bank, the CHRO realized that after more than 10 years of focusing on reducing risk after the 2008 financial crisis, they needed to take more risks and innovate in order to compete in a growing market subject to disruption by fintech firms and cryptocurrencies as well as general industry consolidation. In order to align the culture, the business leader focused on the *obvious* elements by updating the company values and introducing new competencies, including agility, growth mindset, and entrepreneurship.

Sustained

Beyond the *obvious* elements of aligning values and competency models to drive or foster the culture that you want, you can systematically align your culture with greater confidence by paying special attention to the hidden dimensions of culture within the art and science model. Let's revisit how this works.

First, you must develop a clear understanding of the strategy and actions required to enable the culture you want. Beyond communicating the ideal culture, you systematically work the *obvious* and *hidden* dimensions of the model to align the mindsets, behaviors, and systems necessary to embed the culture within the day-to-day work of the organization. Leaders at all levels are then creating a reflection that aligns with the desired, enabling culture.

And importantly, you have done the critical work of auditing and aligning talent systems and critical work practices to embed new thinking (in the form of goals, strategies, and values)—consciously displacing the old (negative, fear-based) thinking from the old culture.

Resilient

Most leaders would consider spending any time in the *aligned* level of maturity—after a culture transformation—to be a major accomplishment. And they would be right. Over the years, we have helped clients make meaningful progress along the culture maturity model, and, in most cases, they were thrilled to make an improvement. In most cases, approaching the *sustained* level of maturity would be considered a homerun.

This would typically include impacts such as dramatic improvements in employee engagement scores, reduction in turnover, reduced cycle times, more innovative ideas, rapid growth in sales and margin, and doubling or tripling market capitalization. Who wouldn't want these things? Those who need to respond to constant changes in the world around them, that's who.

Why build in a full capability to continuously monitor and help your own culture adapt and be as agile as possible? Those who operate in a VUCA world recognize that speed to strategy execution is wholly dependent on positively shifting the hearts and minds of your employees to enable that strategy.

You have built an organizational awareness around a holistic view of culture at the resilient level. By building this awareness throughout your organization, you can continue to monitor and adapt your culture deliberately, intentionally, and purposefully to drive your results.

In organizations at the *resilient* culture capability level:

- You are aware that corporate culture exists and that it impacts your performance.
- You constantly monitor and adjust your culture to align with your business strategy.

- You have defined your ideal culture and measure your progress toward bringing that culture to life.
- You understand the role of thinking and the reflection of your leaders in shaping your culture.
- You share deep feedback with each other about how you are showing up to create the culture.

This enables leaders at all levels to be responsible for maintaining the alignment of your ideal culture to your strategy.

HOW TO TRANSFORM YOUR CULTURE, TEAM BY TEAM

As you prepare to evolve your culture to be more agile, more resilient, and more capable of change (a higher level of culture capability), you will need to leverage a reliable process for transforming cultures. No matter how you approach this work, or who you work with, it needs to be systemic, addressing the whole organization.

We view the systemic approach as a ripple effect at a high level. We start with the executive team and work outward in the organization, team by team, to drive change in work teams. We move teams through our proven DIA-AIM methodology (Figure 5.2).

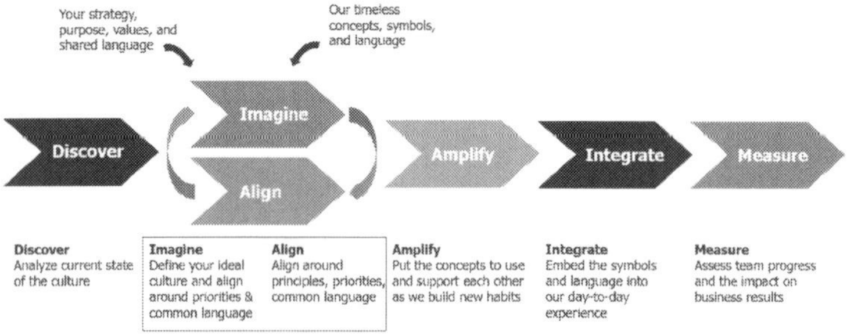

Figure 5.2 DIA-AIM Culture Transformation Methodology.

The first step in our methodology is to *discover* your current culture. Since culture mainly operates from the subconscious mind, it is important to notice it, look at it more objectively, and gather quantitative and qualitative data to help us understand the starting point. At this point, it's not about determining where we want to go, it's about understanding where we are today.

During this phase, we would interview executive team members and key stakeholders, run our Culture Capability Assessment™, and review existing data from people, operating, and financial reports. And, since we need to understand cultural gaps, we also would review the current business strategy, including strategic priorities and initiatives. This will help us start to get an understanding of where the culture is and how it is aligned or not aligned to enable your strategy.

Especially at the executive team level, the subsequent two phases are iterative. While we often get asked at this time to clearly articulate the ideal culture, often through a set of values or principles, we can't yet see them clearly with the client until we go through this iterative process of both imagining the future organization and what we need as well as aligning ourselves as individuals and as a team to that imagined future state.

Again, as Albert Einstein once said, you can't solve a problem from the same level of consciousness you had when you created it. In much the same way, we must go through this iterative process to become more self-aware and aware of our current culture to be able to envision what the ideal state could look like. This will often take a few days and leverage our timeless concepts, symbols, and language in concert with your historical way of communicating about your culture.

Our collection of timeless concepts, symbols, and language help you develop and maintain a healthy state of mind. The principles we apply allow us to efficiently shift mindsets and align actions to better collaborate with each other and enable your strategy. We have built experiential learning exercises around our core models of concepts like *confident vulnerability, a healthy state of mind, how thinking drives results, how to focus our time and energy on what's important, how to remain curious with others,* and so on. These experiences, symbols, and language become psychological anchors that help us develop habits and rapidly rewire our brains for success.

After the iterations are complete, we have a set of aligned definitions and descriptions of our ideal culture. Then it is time to build those into our daily habits and begin to embed them more deeply into the culture of the team and the broader organization. We *amplify* the ideal culture actions in our day-to-day work within our team—sharing feedback with each other on our progress and providing coaching on how we can be even better.

At this point, modeling these behaviors *during our day-to-day work* is essential to building a thriving ideal state culture. Once we begin to model and accept those actions from ourselves, our team, and those around us, we have clearly communicated to the organization what our ideal state should be, and it's time to both engage the next level of leadership as well as begin to *integrate* these ideal actions into our work practices and strategic initiatives.

HOW DO YOU BRING A CULTURE TO LIFE WITHOUT ADDING ANYTHING TO YOUR CALENDAR?

Instead of reaching out to the organization and identifying focus groups, long lists of activities to complete, or setting up a project or program management office and dozens of people to begin to think about how we bring a culture to life, we often challenge leaders to identify ways to bring the culture to life—visibly and quickly—without adding a single thing to their calendars. This request forces the team to look at themselves and their reflection of leadership as the primary mechanism for transforming cultures.

In our sessions, leaders will open their calendars and identify specific opportunities to model the actions they most want to see in the organization. For example, they may want more teamwork and collaboration and notice that they have a cross-functional project team meeting that would allow them to encourage or reward teaming. Leaders might also identify a town hall meeting where they have the opportunity to model what it means to develop a culture of appreciation.

The power of shaping the culture by using existing meetings is that these are the *real* cues that employees follow anyway. Having leaders show up in their day-to-day work is much more powerful than having them act a certain way during a scripted training program.

Finally, it is critical to *measure* your progress. As we discussed earlier, it's important to identify key metrics by which you can monitor and track your progress in developing your organization's ideal culture. You should periodically monitor your progress in these areas to see how far you've come, identify any areas of opportunity where you can be more effective, and reward and recognize those acting in a way that's consistent with your ideal culture.

Why do we need to measure progress? By measuring progress, we help individuals, teams, and organizations create virtuous thought cycles (Figure 5.3) that connect their new thinking with the desired results.

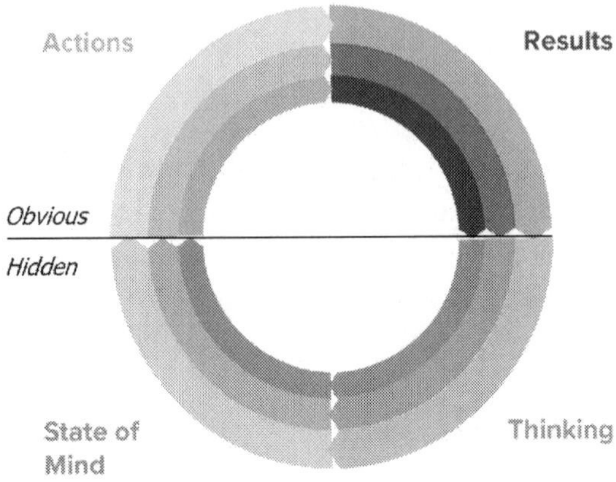

Figure 5.3 Our Thought Cycle can help individuals, teams, and organizations connect thinking to results.

In one large retail organization we worked with, we began to roll out the ideal culture by division and even by district. As we measured and demonstrated the new culture's positive impact, people began associating the ideal culture with the desired results. As districts put the new culture to work, you could see positive improvements in sales, conversion rates (the number of shoppers that purchase during a store visit), customer satisfaction, and even their ability to reduce store associate turnover. Since districts were measured and rewarded based on their performance against these metrics, they began to see transforming their store cultures as a powerful mechanism for getting results.

This Thought Cycle can then create virtuous positive cycles for leaders. They begin to see that new thinking creates healthy states of mind and new actions that generate better results. Those positive results reinforce the thinking and so forth and so on. Once leaders begin to understand the connection between thinking and results, they become more and more committed to changing their actions to better fit the ideal culture of the organization.

WATCH OUT FOR THE HIDDEN TRAPS OF BUILDING CULTURE CAPABILITY

Now that you're on your way to creating the culture you've always wanted and know that you need, here are some hidden traps to watch out for.

Trap #1: Focus on things to *do* instead of how you are *acting*

Too often, clients diagnose their cultures, force-rank the opportunities, and create action plans, task forces, or committees to generate recommendations. Once the recommendations come in, clients tend to find that they all are aligned with the *obvious* elements of culture—those at the top of the iceberg in Figure 2.1. While it's important to have those obvious elements aligned, as we've discussed before, the primary drivers of culture are the hidden elements, including our reflection of leadership.

To avoid this trap, we challenge leaders to drive culture transformation without adding anything to their calendars. How do you drive change then? The answer is both simple and hard: change how you show up in your day-to-day work.

Trap #2: Culture as Initiative

Another common mistake we see is treating culture as an initiative. Your people are your most important assets, and how they act and work together is the lynchpin of your organization's success. Culture, then, is not a separate and time-bound activity. It is the essence of how you do all the activities in work to get results. Culture is about noticing current actions and choosing how you want to act in an ideal situation.

Trap #3: Perfection over speed

In many situations, there is a tendency to want everything to be *perfect* to move forward. We want to wait until everything is perfect before we move ahead. "I am expecting to fill a new role soon," or "We may end up acquiring a company next quarter," or "We need the ideal culture, including values, actions, behaviors, and competencies, clearly defined before we roll this out."

What tends to happen, though in every case is we find there is *no perfect time* to advance your culture. There is always change in large organizations. Moving with speed is your best opportunity to tip the organizational culture toward your ideal state. Would you rather search for a new leader, acquire a new company, or clearly articulate your ideal culture while in a healthy state of mind with aligned colleagues or with a culture that is unhealthy or misaligned with your strategy?

Culture carries with it a great deal of inertia. To shift the collective thinking in an organization, it is important to move with speed to overcome that inertia and embed the new culture you desire.

Trap #4: Disconfirming evidence

We are looking to increase our percentage of successful, ideal actions—our batting average. Although we commit to acting differently, we will undoubtedly slip back to our old autopilot habits at times. If we look at the times we slip back to old habits as evidence that we have failed (rather than times when we are off our game), we can end up breeding cynicism. Alternatively, we can look at our intentions and our batting average for the ideal actions and be inspired by seeing improvements. And, given our mirror neurons and leadership reflection, these improvements can rapidly flow through entire organizations, inspiring transformational change.

"See, I told you they wouldn't be able to be more collaborative!" Looking for people to trip up is perfectly normal. However, this is not a sign that no progress is being made. Rather, it's a perfect opportunity to explore why it happened and what support the person needs to reduce the likelihood of it happening again.

Trap #5: Using common language as weapons vs. tools

Early in our work with a senior team at a technology company, we had them share their commitments of how they want to change. Just a couple of months after the commitments had been made, the CEO led the senior team through a stressful board meeting. The rest of the executive team was then excused before the CEO.

They then began to discuss how the CEO really wasn't listening like he'd said he would. He had been on his phone half the time. As the executives sat around criticizing the CEO for not living up to his commitments using the shared language, one observant (and brave) executive said, "Well, you know we're doing the same thing right now. We said we would assume positive intent with each other, and yet, we are here judging the CEO—and while he's not in the room."

We quickly realized that our states of mind had become unhealthy. When our state of mind is unhealthy, we become very critical of others and can use the shared language as a weapon. When we are in a healthy state of mind, we can ask for feedback, share support, and explore someone's thinking using a shared language. The key is to notice the collective state of mind and speak up! That's the key to using common language as tools (rather than weapons).

Trap #6: Getting out over your skis

Executive teams tend to move through this process first. Sometimes months later, next-level leaders move through a similar process. In larger organizations, there can then sometimes be a perceived lag in moving forward. Unfortunately, this is to be expected.

The experience of becoming more aware of the culture and our individual alignment with it in our thinking and actions is a powerful experience that can lead to real change. But it takes a while to truly engage an entire organization. What we typically see is that when leaders feel that other employees are less engaged with the new culture than they are, they begin telling people to get more engaged. But, telling someone to get more engaged is rarely an effective strategy. Simply telling teams how you want them to change doesn't work, just as telling your children or spouse that you'd like them to change how they act doesn't work.

Be patient and deliberate and stay centered over your skis as you move through transformation. Getting too far out front will slow down the process.

Trap #7: Delegating to HR

Handing over your culture to HR is often the kiss of death. While HR has a significant, even central role in culture transformation, we like to think about HR's role as *leading from the aft*. As you think about mirror neurons and the reflection of leadership, business leaders typically have 95 percent of all employees reporting into them, not into HR. So, driving a culture transformation that involves shifting all employees' actions from HR is not realistic.

You guide and steer the leaders of the organization. You provide frameworks and tools, support the process, and steward the values you wish to see in the teams and the organization—just the way you drive most every change you make in the organization. What is realistic is having HR become the rudder for the process.

At the end of the day, the executive team and top leaders set the tone for the culture—what we do (and don't do) and what we accept (and won't accept) becomes the blueprint for the rest of the organization.

As you begin to see how culture can become a strategic capability for your organization, you can start to leverage this capability to drive results. The more you strengthen the connection between culture and results, the more leaders will become motivated to join in the journey.

KEY TAKEAWAYS

- Culture capability is a strategic skill that will enable you to continue to adapt to external markets and align your organization internally.
- Culture capability can be developed over time: the Culture Capability Maturity Model provides a blueprint to diagnose not only your current level of capability, but also a clear vision for how to advance.
- There is a proven methodology to transform culture: the DIA-AIM provides a powerful and efficient process for aligning teams to the ideal culture.
- Beware the common traps that can slow down or undermine your culture transformation, including the use of leaders tripping up as disconfirming evidence.

QUESTIONS TO CONSIDER

- As you look across your organization, what level of culture capability exists, and how might that enable or inhibit your strategic priorities?
- What methods have you tried in the past to reliably change the habits of adults?
- How might you use the DIA-AIM model to align your team's actions to the organization's values?
- What are the common traps that show up in your organization during similar transformations? What more can you do to help remove them so the culture transformation can be successful?
- What would you do differently if you needed to transform your culture without adding one thing to your calendar?

CHAPTER 6
PRINCIPLES OF CULTURE TRANSFORMATION

Change your thoughts and you change your world.

NORMAN VINCENT PEALE

How much control do leaders have over the pace of culture change? This brief story illustrates the point.

Chad was having a conversation with the CEO of a global convenience store chain—at its corporate headquarters. He and the CEO had attended the same business school and the CEO graciously agreed to meet and explore common areas of interest.

As Chad listened to him talk about his 11 years leading the organization, the CEO eventually turned to Chad and asked what he specialized in. When Chad mentioned culture, the CEO said he had been working on culture transformation since he took over and felt he hadn't made as much progress as he would have liked.

We often hear statements like this. In fact, when we hear this statement, it is frequently coupled with frustration painted on the faces of leaders of companies who can't seem to get their arms around improving their cultures.

DOES CULTURE TRANSFORMATION REALLY TAKE AT LEAST 18 MONTHS?

And then there are the even more frustrated leaders who, upon getting their board's blessing to initiate a transformation effort, would hear that their project would take "at least eighteen months" or "two to three years." As many executive roles only last for three years, culture initiatives often turn into more of a legacy effort versus a strategic capability to help executives get immediate business results. And, because of a common limiting belief—that culture transformation takes more versus less time—leaders are skeptical that they will be able to transform cultures more quickly.

In fact, at one large technology organization we worked with, the company executive who led the transformation bet us that they would see no difference until six months into the process. We took the bet. And that bet was paid out about a week after the six-month period when that executive returned from another office in a foreign country and told us, "It's even better over there!"

There is no one-size-fits-all timeline for culture change. The conventional wisdom that it takes eighteen months to make a noticeable change to your organization's culture is just a limiting belief. As you may have experienced, getting a new CEO, being sold to a private equity firm, going through an IPO, winning a huge contract, and other major events can seemingly change the culture overnight. But, when you don't *intentionally* shape your culture, it often just creeps along.

The good news? *You* are in control of the pace of your culture change, and you can create the change you desire at the pace that works best for your organization. We can confidently say that because we have evidence it is possible.

YOU CAN CHANGE YOUR CULTURE AS QUICKLY AS YOU CAN CHANGE YOUR MIND(SET)

As we've seen firsthand, changing cultures has everything to do with changing mindsets. It's hard to change mindsets quickly, right? Not necessarily. You may have noticed that some people change seemingly overnight from significant emotional events.[1] Think about getting married or divorced, having your first child, becoming an empty-nester, or having a near-death experience. These significant experiences can dramatically shift how we see the world, our thinking, and our behaviors. And, the change can come very quickly.

One corporate CEO with whom we had done business shared with us his riveting near-death experience. He was in a terrible automobile accident in the early 1990s. He found himself injured, scared, and alone for quite a while. During this time, he realized that while he had accumulated lots of money, he couldn't take it with him, and he had used very little of that to bring good to others in the world.

Shortly after he recovered, he donated millions to a local university and similar amounts to a local medical center. He then started a philanthropic organization with his wife to begin to give back and help society.

How long does personal change take? It can be instant. We've seen it happen hundreds of times. And all it takes is a slight shift in your mindset to change how you see the world.

WHAT KIND OF PERSONAL CHANGE IS REQUIRED TO RADICALLY TRANSFORM CULTURES?

In many leaders, we see anxiety about their personal changes because they make change out to be more than is required.

Instead of changing who you are as a leader, the wiser choice is to start by just making a slight shift in *how* you are *being*.

You may be surprised by how small shifts in how leaders act can radically transform organizational cultures. Here are some examples of small shifts that happen at the top of organizations to dramatically transform their cultures:

- A CEO offered to let his senior team play a bigger role in strategic, organization-wide initiatives, and the whole organization became more collaborative.
- A president shared a vulnerable story about her uncertainty regarding her confidence as she faced the COVID-19 crisis. As a result of her vulnerability, her 8,000-person organization stepped forward and delivered remarkable business results.
- The CEO of a large retail organization shared that he isn't always personally accountable, and his 100,000 associates began to ask what more they could do to be more accountable and get results.
- A healthcare CEO began to ask more open-ended questions from her administrators and, as a result, built higher levels of trust across her hospitals and divisions.

As we begin our engagements, we ask senior team members what they value most about how their leaders lead and what they feel they could do to make an even more positive impact on the organization. Most are not surprised by the themes when we bring their feedback to the CEOs. They respond matter-of-factly with a statement to the effect of, "Yes, I've heard that feedback throughout my career."

After our senior team alignment session, we ask our CEO clients to commit to making minor improvements in just one area of their organization. Those improvements often have to do with giving more autonomy to senior team members, such as listening more, asking more questions, providing more feedback and coaching, or focusing the team's energy and attention on a few critical priorities that will add the most value to the organization.

As CEOs and other leaders commit to making some progress in each of the above areas after shifting their mindsets in an alignment session, they can begin to make progress—and that progress gets noticed, appreciated, and amplified throughout the organization. Their thinking that a slight improvement can and will make a considerable difference provides momentum for them to sustain the change they commit to make.

A large retailer client had rolled out a new labor forecasting and scheduling tool for over 200,000 associates. Upon visiting their stores, the executive team noticed that their associates were not using their expensive labor system to better align associate hours to the times when more customers would be shopping.

After exploring *why* it still makes sense for the stores to focus more on visual standards than labor scheduling, the executives realized that *all* of their store visits started with 30 minutes of nit-picking the visual standards in front of the store they were visiting. Suddenly, it became apparent that the executives' actions were sending the wrong message to the store leaders.

During the next store visit, the executive team started the discussion with the store leaders *in the back* of the store by asking about the labor schedules. The store leaders quickly adjusted, now noticing that the executives emphasized how the store was staffed (as opposed to the visual standards). The visit reinforced for the store leaders that labor scheduling was a critical focus for the executives. Before the executives arrived at the next store, the store leaders called ahead to warn them that the executives would be asking about the labor schedules. So, the next store leadership team was ready in advance.

Just a few more store visits started at the back and the district and region managers had the *news* spread across the nation to several thousand stores: "Executive visits will start in the back and focus on labor scheduling." And, just like that, we successfully shifted the thinking and habits of 200,000 associates.

HOW CAN YOU SYSTEMATICALLY SHAPE AND QUICKEN YOUR CULTURE CHANGE OR TRANSFORMATION?

A leader acting with intention is an important element of shifting cultures. But it's clearly not the only one. We have discovered five levers to be fundamental principles of culture transformation that help significantly accelerate culture success (Figure 6.1). These principles are continuously operating on and in your culture, and whether you are aware of them or not, they exist.

It's much like the process of flying a plane. The principles of flight including lift, weight, thrust, and drag are always acting on the plane (whether you are aware of them, or not) and together they shape the experience of flight.

THE FIVE PRINCIPLES OF SUCCESSFUL CULTURE TRANSFORMATION

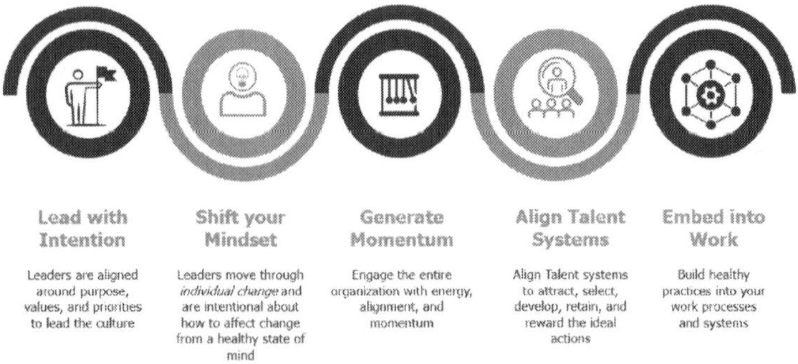

Figure 6.1 The Five Principles of Successful Culture Transformation.

Over the years, these five *hidden* principles emerged as the fundamental levers to drive culture transformation. When they were all in place, transformations were accelerated and sustained. The most effective leaders we know have the ability to thread the five principles throughout the transformation process, moving quickly from ideas to action.

Transformation can occur at a very intense pace when actions are in sync with these principles, and high performance can be attained. However, when these principles are not honored or are violated, transformation is stalled, and performance is sub-optimized. Let's take a deeper look at each one.

PRINCIPLE #1: LEAD WITH INTENTION

Most leaders know that Intentional leadership must start at the top of the organization, with the CEO and executive team. What is less understood are the tenets of intentional leadership. Everyone needs to be clear about the purpose, strategies, and plans of action. Clarity around these elements is noticed by the mirror neurons of everyone in the organization.

The only purpose of mirror neurons is to notice the behaviors of others around us—and they are especially attuned to leadership behavior. What this means in practical terms is that as a result, communications are simpler to understand, clearer, and more consistent. When it feels like we're "rowing in the same direction," mirror neurons are firing.

That sense of rhythm, energy, and confidence only occurs when the CEO and executive team are aligned and moving forward in the same direction. This alignment provides a clear path and purpose for the rest of the organization to follow. This is because the CEO leads the broadest culture in the organization.

Working on one subculture within a department, function, or division will inevitably be influenced by the broader culture, and changes will generally revert to the broadest culture. And to be clear, it doesn't mean that everyone is in lockstep obedience. Rather, it means that there is instead a shared vision for the business and beliefs about how that vision will be accomplished.

The importance of shared experience, common language, symbols, and stories

As you begin to lead your culture as an aligned leadership team, it will be important to align the rest of your organization to your thinking and direction. The following are the important elements that can help you more quickly align your organization to your new culture:

- **Shared experience**: To shift your thinking, you need experience to help you notice your subconscious behaviors and, as a result, choose better behaviors in your conscious minds as you develop new, healthier habits. Since leader-led natural work teams are the primary social reinforcement, you should have these experiences as an intact team so that everyone commits to change and supports the change back on the job.
- **Common language**: Language is a powerful mechanism for representing what we believe is most important in our culture. Having a common way you talk about your culture will clearly communicate to your colleagues what is important and accepted. For example, saying that you are "a team together and a team apart" can present powerful language for unifying an executive team.
- **Shared symbols**: For most of recorded history, we have used symbols to convey meaning about abstract ideas of concepts. In culture transformation, we use symbols introduced during shared experiences to quickly bring the team back to a healthy state. For instance, we have a

symbol to remind us to stay *in touch* with the people most important to us: our customers, patients, or colleagues. With a quick glance at the symbol for *in touch,* we return to our best selves, notice what people need, and choose the behaviors we ideally want to drive our performance.

- **Stories**: Stories are an important way to share *confident vulnerability* as we lead culture transformations. They help people relate to us and see the possibility for them to change. A few well-placed stories can help illuminate the common language and symbols we use to align cultures.

For example, in a large consumer company, the senior leadership team went through an alignment session to better understand how they were showing up—the good news and things they could do better. As they spoke at a town hall meeting, they took turns showing up on stage or on video, sharing those strengths and the things they were working on. As the next 200 leaders watched the executives share, they were inspired to learn more about themselves—including how they could also be more effective.

PRINCIPLE #2: SHIFT YOUR MINDSET

Albert Einstein was right: you simply can't solve problems from the same level of consciousness you had when you created them. You must increase your awareness of your thinking and state of mind to understand why you act the way you do. That's the key. Once you notice your thinking and state of mind, you can move through personal change.

All change is biological and happens at the individual level: in our nervous systems, emotions, confidence to act or lack of it. Individuals must change to create a different culture within a team or organization, starting with the CEO. Too often, we see leaders asking *their organizations* to change. That suggests that the leader isn't ready for personal change and that reflection of leadership will reverberate within their organization: "I'm not ready for personal change."

The net result from no individual change is no culture change.

What more can we learn? How else might we approach this? What can we change to be even more effective? One CEO we knew ended most conversations by saying, "Let's just go learn something." Instead, when leaders display a growth mindset and a sense of confident vulnerability, their organizations are quick to follow. This kind of openness lights a fire that spreads throughout the entire organization—the energy needed to drive rapid individual change at scale.

PRINCIPLE #3: GENERATE MOMENTUM

Once you are more open to personal change, you must work to generate positive energy and momentum in your organization to shift the organizational culture. Why? Because all organizations have built *antibodies* into their cultures. By this, we mean that their limiting beliefs and habits reject the very things they need the most.

For example, organizations that are always "too busy" with meetings and work will not "have time" to address culture change. Organizations that are plagued by more of a "fixed mindset" and feel they already know what they need to know will not bring in the "specialized expertise" often required to drive change. Organizations that cannot "make decisions" quickly will put off and pass around whether or not to focus on their culture until it is "too late" to adjust to enable their current strategy.

In one sales meeting with a large oil and gas company, we walked the leader through our process and methodology. The leader quickly noticed the problems in her team, including a lack of alignment. After we provided a proposal, we checked back in with her in a couple of weeks. She said she wanted to move ahead but needed to check with her team to get their buy-in and support.

We remarked, "You mean that team we just talked about had trouble getting aligned?" As a leader, you can sometimes see what's wrong, but when you turn it back to the group, the antibodies can quickly take over and prevent the change you need.

To overcome this internal resistance built into the system, you will need to overwhelm the current culture with the language, symbols, felt behaviors, and the visible signs of a new culture by generating momentum and positive energy.

Generating energy throughout an organization is best accomplished by impacting leaders with their working teams—including "linking" roles. Rensis Likert originally put forward this concept in the 1960s, and it describes how work groups are connected by members (often leaders) who participate in multiple groups and serve as "connectors."[2] Imagine a CFO who participates in the executive committee and the finance leadership team. By mapping out these key roles and intact work groups, you can begin to see how to quickly align leaders throughout your organization.

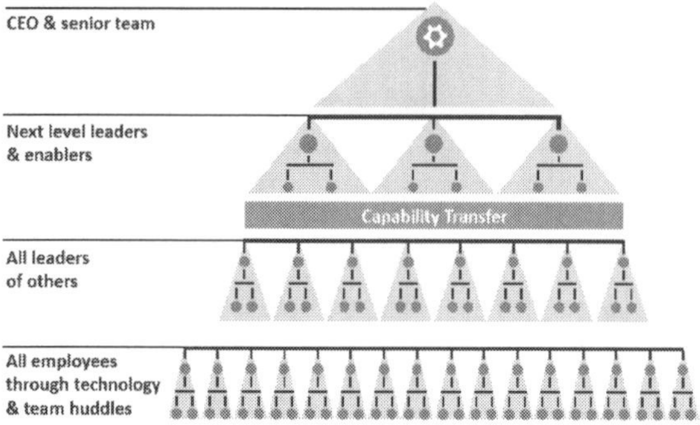

Figure 6.3 Generating alignment at scale through Likert's *linking pin* model.

The links in the chain in Figure 6.3 help you generate and maintain alignment as you move quickly through change by modeling the right actions and monitoring and providing feedback to those around them.

Another critical element of generating alignment at scale is to ensure that the common language and symbols you use have a shared understanding. Too often, we see the tops of organizations using either "corporate" or "consultant" language to communicate their ideal culture. Phrases like "act like an owner" mean very little to folks who have never owned or operated a business—or even supervised anyone.

To check for alignment, we often leverage focus groups or virtual focus groups with up to 1,000 concurrent users leveraging an AI platform to help us understand what is resonating and unclear. For example, in a large IT organization, we developed a set of leadership behaviors to define the culture and found that when employees were asked to describe what each one meant, there was clarity around four of the five behaviors.

The fifth was akin to "act like a founder," and when asked what it meant, many typed "I don't know" or "no idea." Developing a shared understanding of the common symbols and language is simple to do and absolutely critical to aligning organizational culture.

Since culture is aligned with strategy and culture transformation impacts all other strategic initiatives in an organization, it is critical to connect and integrate it to all your critical initiatives. Too often, organizations treat culture as an initiative on its own. Let's work on that and then get back to work. In our experience, you can generate tremendous momentum when you power your critical initiatives with the key elements of your new culture.

PRINCIPLE #4: ALIGN TALENT SYSTEMS

To sustain your new culture, you must align your talent systems to reinforce and reward your desired culture. If you select *win-lose* leaders and then ask them to function as a *win-win*, you will always be fighting their innate tendencies. If you reward and compensate executives for the way *their division performs,* good luck trying to get them to focus on the *organization's greater good.*

With one of our favorite clients, we held an annual working session with the executive team nearly two years into a remarkable culture transformation. Pleased with many of the areas that were advancing, the one place the CEO identified wanting to see even more progress was having his team members collaborate and work on broader corporate goals. After working first on developing a positive state of mind within the team, we opened a discussion around what barriers could be getting in the way.

The president of the largest division shared that more than 90 percent of his annual compensation was tied to the success of this division. He also suggested that he would be willing to move more of his bonus to be determined by broader company objectives. The rest of the team agreed to make that shift, which involved aligning their talent systems more closely to reward the behaviors they wanted to see in the culture. It was a tangible step that made a huge difference.

Aligning systems doubled revenue

A leader of a medical devices company quickly picked up on the importance of aligning talent systems to culture. The strategy included the need to double their revenue, but he promptly identified their compensation systems for sales were fundamentally flawed and could never double.

Once he built up the organizational health (state of mind), he was able to restructure the organization and its comp model to encourage more collaboration. That was the fundamental force that drove the culture change and enabled them to double revenue from $2 billion to $4 billion in two years.

Anixter's *Blue Book:* Preserving culture through dramatic growth

Founded by Alan and Bill Anixter in 1957 with a $20,000 investment, this wire and cable distribution company went from the Midwest version of a garage—a single warehouse—to become a $6 billion leading global distributor of network and security solutions, electrical and electronic solutions, and utility power solutions.

In 2021 Anixter went through its second acquisition by Wesco to form a $18 billion distribution services company. Today the company helps build, connect, protect, and power valuable assets and critical infrastructures. Ask any of Anixter's 6,000-plus employees worldwide what made the company successful, and most will say without hesitation, "the culture."

Anixter's profoundly entrepreneurial sales culture was summarized early on in a simple little booklet called *The Blue*

Book. Its origins became company lore. When the Anixters went to apply for their first significant loan in 1967, the bankers asked them to bring their policy manual along. They didn't have one. So, they took an irreverent book they loved, *Up the Organization* by Robert Townsend, the founder of Avis. Its subtitle, *How to Stop Stifling People and Strangling Profits*, and overall irreverence, perfectly captured their ethos.[3]

They put a blue cover on it entitled Anixter Policy Manual and took it to the meeting at the bank. It was only after they were successful in getting the loan that one of the bankers asked to see their "policy manual." They slid it across the desk and he opened it, took one look at the table of contents, then satisfied, closed the book. They had pulled off a small charade but also a bigger statement of who they were and weren't as company.

Their third in command, Bruce Van Wagner, then wrote an even briefer statement of their values which, in the simplest of language, spelled out the fundamental principles that defined the way the company operated: *The Anixter Way*.

The following are some of the key principles that defined Anixter's culture and have lasted for 60 years of incredible growth, from $20,000 to $6 billion (just prior to acquisition by Wesco):

- *People* is the first word in our business philosophy—and the last.
- Think! Think often, think hard, and then say what you think.
- We cannot afford the luxury of a poor day's business.
- Our word is our bond—we are reliable.
- Customers are not dependent on us. We're dependent on them.
- Enthusiasm is the greatest business asset in the world. It beats money, power, and influence.

- Enthusiasm is contagious, so carry it in your attitude and manner. It will increase productivity and bring joy and satisfaction to our people.
- Each one of us must pay for ourselves each year.
- Tellingly, both "organization charts" and "job descriptions" were intentionally left blank, signifying a real trust that if they hired smart people, they would help grow the company.

It's not that those things didn't exist. It was more the defining spirit of trust that enabled Anixter's meteoric growth.

The Anixter *Blue Book* is now in its 32nd printing in a dozen languages. It became genetic code, not just part of onboarding, training, and expansion but present in everyday conversations. As Julie Anixter, Bill's daughter, who led training and learning systems at the company for over a decade, put it, the *Blue Book* "was in the water system." Five CEOs in succession honored and leveraged it to ensure that, as the company grew, they maintained the "service is our technology" ethos and culture they needed, which truly set them apart.[4]

PRINCIPLE #5: EMBED INTO WORK

Work practices reflect our thinking at the time the processes were developed. Oftentimes, work practices lag behind strategy and are years or even decades old. In many situations, companies who ask for more collaboration have processes that run through only one department—asking another only for approval.

When thinking is embedded into work, our good intentions to shift our behaviors and relationships with others are hindered by the behaviors required by tasks outlined in our processes. Thus, our old thinking is still locked into the system, confining us to "the way it works around here."

In a large retail organization, the marketing department created a brand persona, a fictitious character created by a retailer to mimic a real customer. This persona was quite elaborate, describing thinking, lifestyle, habits, interests, hobbies, and more —down to the details.

To help bring this persona to life for customers through the stores and store associates, the president of stores met with the marketing department to better understand the brand persona. She was informed that the brand persona was a highly guarded trade secret and could be shared only with the CEO and the marketing leadership team. The language, symbols, and stories were under lock and key.

In this example, you can clearly see how embedded thinking exists in work processes. If your culture is about collaboration and inclusion, but your team's processes don't include collaboration—even around critical elements to unlock your strategy—you are not likely to see the teamwork you really need to drive success.

BEWARE THE TRAP OF DISCONFIRMING EVIDENCE

As you commit to your new culture (personally and as a team), you will undoubtedly experience times in living the new behaviors and times where one or more old/dysfunctional behaviors show up. After all, we are still human beings. So, it is important to remember to set this expectation and get alignment *up front* from your leaders. Otherwise, this will slow down your culture transformation.

We often meet with a senior team a month or more after their shared experience, and someone will say something like, "The CEO was back to herself this morning," or "I knew Mary couldn't keep behaving this way." We call this *looking for disconfirming evidence*. It's a natural thing to do and part of the scientific method of analyzing data. *Is there any evidence that would disconfirm this finding?*

Yet when we apply this standard to human beings, whom we know experience healthy and unhealthy states of mind and can operate from their subconscious minds that have been programmed over a lifetime, it simply becomes an excuse not to move forward with a transformation.

But there is a solution, and that is to look for *progress* over *perfection*. Here, think of the times you spend in a healthy state of mind. These are times when your actions match your intentions. You are doing what you said you wanted to do. Consider these states of well-being to be like a baseball player's *batting average*.

The Major League Baseball (MLB) batting average in the United States is approximately .260. This number is out of 1.0, so a .260 batting average is equivalent to getting a hit and on base 26 percent of the time. So, essentially here, we celebrate hitters who are unsuccessful 74 percent of the time. Said another way, the average MLB player will fail to get on base for the overwhelming majority of his entire career.

Now let's look at the best baseball players—those admitted to the MLB Hall of Fame. They must be exceptional batters, right? Well, not really. Their batting average is just over .300, meaning they only get on base 30 percent of the time (and fail to do so 70 percent of the time). Take Ty Cobb, a Hall of Famer, who holds the record for the highest career batting average at .366. Yet his average reflects that he still failed to get on base for the overwhelming majority of his career.

Looking at our actions through the lens of a *batting average* as we did above helps us begin to see how culture transformation occurs. Each and every time you choose to act differently as a leader, you are noticed by the mirror neurons of dozens if not hundreds of your peers in your organization. The small shift you made is conveyed through stories about your success to countless others.

Once your culture-transformation stakeholders hear a few times that "we are pivoting from cost-cutting to top-line growth" and see you follow through in your actions, others rapidly spread the word through their formal and informal networks. Eventually, these stories or your leadership develops into a new narrative inside your company. Then, when the change team starts aligning values, behaviors, and systems with these stories and actions—talent and operational—all of your *oars* start and continue pulling in the same direction—focused on growth.

KEY TAKEAWAYS

- Culture transformation starts by shifting leader actions—your reflection of leadership.
- The five principles of culture transformation are always at work in your organization: how you lead, your collective mindsets, building momentum, aligning your talent systems, and embedding into work processes.
- Culture transformation is best scaled using Likert's linking pin model—connecting the CEO to the front line through intact teams.
- Transforming culture is a game of incremental changes in your actions. We are seeking improvement, not perfection. Think about your ability to change your leadership *batting average* over time.

QUESTIONS TO CONSIDER

- What feedback have you had as a leader over your career (positive and constructive)? How might your tendencies be reflected in the actions you see in those around you?
- What do you notice about the relationship between how your senior team behaves and how the organization tends to operate?
- What do your current talent systems reward? Enterprise wins or individual success? Taking risks or playing it safe? Innovation or operating to plan? Are these what you need to enable your strategy?
- Which of the five principles of culture transformation are operating to your advantage and which are missing or holding you back?

CHAPTER 7
WHEN CHANGE SLOWS, LOOK FOR HIDDEN ELEMENTS

Learning and change are biological phenomena.

ALAN SIELER

Focusing only on the *obvious* elements of culture assumes that resistance to change can be overcome through *intellectual debate* and *rational actions*. Let's state the purpose and goals more clearly. Let's revise the compensation system to better align with our goals. Let's have a town hall to articulate the business case for the change. Let's detail the specific behaviors we want to see.

While the *obvious* approaches to culture transformation are necessary to perform at the highest levels, we find them to be woefully insufficient on their own. For example, we are often called in by executives who have done an exceptional job of articulating shared values that align with their strategies, only to find that people are not living them. In a sense, by painting the values on the walls, the values become wallpaper. By that, we mean that while people work in sight of their stated values daily, they don't notice or live them.

While leaders have the best of intentions in these situations, their actions sometimes make things worse. When values are clearly stated but not lived by leaders, people experience increased levels of frustration and cynicism and develop high levels of resistance to change in the organization.

The ability to fully overcome resistance to change lies in the *hidden* side of organizational culture. Understanding this side of the equation enables leaders to create environments of psychological safety, be mindful of not overwhelming employees, and maximize the impact of their leadership and its influence on the culture.

To better understand how to overcome resistance to change, let's explore why people, leaders included, resist change in the first place. There are two starting points on the hidden side of culture to help us understand: social psychology and neuroscience.

THE ROLE OF ANXIETY IN CHANGE

In our experience, people tend to change when they believe it is in their best interest to change. That is when they move toward something they perceive as more desirable or move away from a potential threat. In other words, people change when their perception of the alternatives available is judged *better* than their current situation.[1] This tends to apply at the individual, team, and organizational levels.

Kurt Lewin, a social psychologist, observed that human systems establish an equilibrium naturally, and change occurs only when the equilibrium is disrupted.[2] How do you create disruption but do so in a manner that is healthy and encourages higher levels of performance? Schein also observes that when discussing true transformational change, the process is more about unlearning than learning something new. The unlearning part of the equation is often overlooked.

Schein suggests that learning and unlearning are a function of balancing two types of anxiety: survival anxiety and learning anxiety. In transformation, we describe this as the balance between the desire to change and the fear of failure. The interaction and awareness of these two different kinds of anxieties create a dynamic that renders either successful change or resistance to change.

The *desire to change* is the motivation that is created by knowing we can do better. Generally, it recognizes that individuals, teams, and organizations can and should perform at higher levels. If we are going to survive and thrive, we must perform at higher levels. Organization members can often identify how they could be more effective, day in and day out.

On the other side of the equation is the *fear of failure*. This is the anxiety created by the need to know and do something new and different. Learning something new takes energy and requires work, and we often aren't sure we'll succeed. Unlearning something creates discomfort. Although the case for change, the threat in the environment, is clear, the fear of learning something new, being a beginner or worse, being incompetent, being punished, or losing status or identity, prevents people from changing.

We have noticed this fear of learning often triggers lower levels of accountability and IMpowerment and ego defenses such as denial, blaming, and excuses, which place individuals and teams into unhealthy states of mind.

OUR DESIRE TO CHANGE MUST BE STRONGER THAN OUR FEAR OF FAILURE

Effective change happens when the *desire to change* is greater than the *fear of failure*. If people can learn a new skill or operate in a new way or way of being with less discomfort and effort than they are experiencing from survival anxiety, they are more likely to make the change.

Imagine a balance scale with *desire to change* on one platform and *fear of failure* on the other (Figure 7.1). For change to happen, the scale has to tip to the *desire to change* side. If the scale tips to the *fear of failure* side, no change will happen, or change will be ephemeral and not last.

Figure 7.1 Change requires the desire to change to be greater than the fear of failure.

We typically see organizations overwhelmed by the desire to change with the fear of failure. The new way of doing something is so complex and takes so many steps that organization members fear that they will fail. Fear of failure could be fear that you don't know what you are doing, that you will be punished for not knowing, or that you could destroy group dynamics and lose connections to the broader team.

TIPPING THE BALANCE IN FAVOR OF CHANGE

To overcome resistance to change, we can tip the balance to increase the *desire to change* and decrease the *fear of failure*. One way to reduce fear of failure is to create psychological safety.[3] At its core, culture change is shifting mindsets and thinking about the current ways people perceive, think, and act.

As psychologists refer to it, this cognitive redefinition[4] is possible only if there is enough psychological safety so that people can individually and collectively learn new and different ways. It's why the "learning organization" movement of the 1980s and '90s was embraced.

Schein was a significant influence on Peter Senge, whose seminal book, *The Learning Organization*, influenced organizations from the US military to Ford, Shell Oil, and the Coca-Cola Company and reinforced the need to create a learning culture.[5] A culture of learning makes it explicit that continuous learning takes place through adopting new behaviors that encourage:

- Trial and error: inventing your own solutions or iterating others
- Practice: reference flight simulators
- Imitation: imitating solutions of another or a role model (through our *reflection of leadership* by mirror neurons)[6]
- Dialogue[7]
- Psychological safety to support these behaviors

Let's look at how this plays out at even the senior-most levels of large organizations.

HOW A CEO'S FEAR PREVENTED HIM FROM COACHING HIS TEAM

While working with the executive team of a large services organization, we were helping the team get better at sharing feedback. During the activity, the team shared that they'd like to have even more feedback from the CEO. When the CEO heard this request from leader after leader on his team, he reflected on why he didn't share more feedback.

While they each thought it was because he was too busy, he shared: "I actually don't share much feedback with each of you because I don't think I'm very good at sharing feedback." The room got quiet. He went on to say that each of them led substantial organizations and that he felt they were terrific coaches. By comparison, he thought he led just the small leadership team and would not provide much helpful feedback.

The team then shared that they deeply respected and valued his input and that he helped each of them become the leaders they are. This allowed the CEO to overcome his anxiety and move forward to become the coach they needed.

In understanding what it takes to learn new things, reduce fear of failure, and continue to answer the question, "Why is it so hard to introduce change?" there are some excellent explanations if we look at the neuroscience of how the brain works.

ALL CHANGE HAPPENS WITHIN THE NERVOUS SYSTEM

Over the last twenty years, neuroscientists have made tremendous gains in integrating psychology and understanding the physiology of the brain. Enabled by advances in imagining technologies and computer analysis, we have a still incomplete but much more robust understanding of how the brain links with the mind. Understanding this link has tremendous implications for leaders of organizations, especially regarding "easing the trauma of human transition."

Here are several neuroscience findings that help us better understand change and how the brain responds to change:

- Change takes effort: work uses energy and creates discomfort.
- Amygdala trip: It is easy to create inaction.
- All change is biological: Neuroplasticity is the key to lasting change.
- Flavor of month: Learning how to stall (or "ice the puck").

Change takes effort

Change takes effort and creates physiological discomfort, which suggests a natural tendency to resist change. This is consistent with the previous discussion of the types of anxiety created with change.

This understanding starts in the working memory of the brain, where new information and ideas are held. This is where your conscious attention leads you to new perceptions. For example, imagine you are in a company meeting or town hall and hear information you have not heard before. You will most likely compare the new information in your working memory against what you already know. This kind of memory activates the cortex, a very energy-intensive part of your brain. The takeaway here is that dealing with new things requires energy.

Evolution has provided us with an energy-saving device, as we learn new things. The learnings are pushed from the cerebral cortex to the basal ganglia to conserve energy. In contrast, the deeper part of the basal ganglia operates very well without conscious thought. Your basal ganglia house the neural networks where long-term habits are formed. It links the parts of the brain to create behaviors based on previous life experiences.

This enables the basal ganglia to use less energy than working memory. As a result, even complex activities like riding a bicycle can become routine and even unconscious.

Remember the amount of energy and focus it took to learn to ride a bike? You had to balance the bike. You needed a source of propulsion in the form of pedaling, which had to be done while you were balancing. You had to turn the wheel and brake. Most importantly, you had to watch out for cars and other vehicles.

After a few months of riding a bicycle, most people can typically ride without thinking. They will experience this phenomenon for years into the future. This is why you can get on a bike and ride it even though you may not have ridden in years. The common saying, "It's like riding a bicycle," implies that it's something learned so deeply that you never entirely forget it.

The same dynamics come into play when we face change and stress in the workplace. Much of what we do in organizations is based on routines and habits. Once in place and hardwired, this automatic pilot requires quite a bit of effort to overcome. This effort makes many of us feel uncomfortable, and as a result, we tend to avoid change.

To overcome this resistance, leaders must be deliberate, intentional, and purposeful in thought and action. With effort, this focus can enable leaders to overcome the inertia of the collectively learned thought habits of the group. They must recognize their autopilot but use it to guide the group toward productive action. The autopilot must not run the show. Once this deliberate change takes hold, it is our experience that success breeds success. Others in the organization learn from and adapt new thinking and actions. The transformation becomes contagious.

To illustrate this, the CEO of a large oil and gas producer wanted to build a sense of one team across the organization and wanted to increase the ownership of the leadership team, which consisted of about 30 vice presidents. The CEO observed, "I pay these individuals very well, yet they wait to be told to do things. In this environment, I need people who know the business and bring me new ideas. I can't possibly know all aspects of this business."

One of the consultants asked, "Do you have any idea why this leadership team waits to be told?" The CEO said, "No." The consultant responded, "My thought is it is exactly what they have been trained to do."

As we learned more about this client, the previous CEO had built a beautiful, sprawling campus with separate buildings for each function and division. This meant that individuals rarely left their part of the campus, much less their building. This is precisely what the previous CEO wanted. He saw himself as the "hub" of the wheel with spokes to each division. He made the decisions, and others executed the work.

This is why the vice presidents, along with the entire organization, waited to be told. They were perfectly trained to do this.

Following an executive alignment session that we held with the top 30 leaders, the CEO recognized that it would take leadership work to overcome these deep-seated thought and behavior patterns. He began asking more questions authentically. He challenged people to bring new and better ideas and resisted giving answers even when it clearly was what needed to be done. He opened decisions to broader groups of people and elicited their ideas. And most importantly, he enlisted the help of his C-suite to engage in similar ideas and actions.

The C-suite decided to advance the transformation by having everyone in the organization participate in a culture alignment session. Of particular note, the CAO of this organization became a facilitator of these sessions. He led discussions, asked questions, clarified expectations, and most importantly, modeled the exact "go forward" behaviors expected in the organization.

We've seen this play out countless times: at a global bank, a large utility, a global retailer, a large consulting firm, a medical devices company, an alternative energy company, etc. A leader changes the way she approaches the organization, enlists her leadership team, engages the next level of leaders to cascade the change, and reinforces the elements of the transformation at every level.

Our clients experience the same type of transition. At first, it takes a fair amount of leadership focus and work, but once the "flywheel" turns several times, the transformation creates energy and change of its own and the organization experiences a multitude of positive "knock-on" effects. While these organizations might initially focus on greater alignment and sense of ownership, like the oil company above, they also begin to see improved collaboration and communication, more employee engagement, more innovation and new ideas, increased customer focus, etc., which form the foundation for improved operational and financial results.

Back to the oil company example, six months after starting the transformation effort, a vice president said, "This is a different place to work. My ideas are welcomed, and I am comfortable seeking out my peers' ideas That would have never happened before. In addition, I can point to several examples of teams delivering projects with real savings because of this work. These were simple changes that we would have missed before."

One year after starting the transformation, the CEO said, "This transformation effort has not only allowed us to survive the previous year, but it has also provided us with a platform to thrive moving forward. My team is different. The vice presidents are different, and the energy in the entire organization is now positive and engaged."

Amygdala trip

In his book *Emotional Intelligence,* Daniel Goleman coined the term "amygdala hijack."[8] The amygdala is the emotional part of the brain. As Goleman states, "Emotions make us pay attention right now." The emotional brain can process information in milliseconds faster than other parts of the brain.

When the sense organs receive information, the stimuli are routed to the thalamus. The thalamus is directly wired to the amygdala, which receives part of the stimuli. The rest of the stimuli are sent to the neocortex or more rational side. The hippocampus then interrupts the stimuli and tells the amygdala whether a threat is present.

The amygdala issues a fight, flight, or freeze response if danger is sensed. This response is almost immediate and often does not match the actual threat level. In other words, the perceived threat is often greater than the actual threat. The amygdala hijacks the ability of the brain to think rationally.

During times of change, we regularly witness leaders taking actions that hijack organization members' amygdalae. We use the term that leaders "trip" the amygdala much like energy surges trip circuit breakers in houses. Circuit breakers are automatic switches installed to protect electrical circuits from damage caused by excess energy. When circuit breakers are tripped, they cut off all electrical power to the circuit.

A similar thing happens in organizations. Leaders have the best intentions to get the organization excited about change but communicate in a way that scares organization members. Often the leaders don't even recognize that this has happened.

An amygdala trip has three responses (that you undoubtedly know well): fight, flight, or freeze. Evolutionarily, these responses were critical to our survival as a species. If we were threatened, we would flee from the situation. If we could not run, we could stand and fight. If the threat was so extreme and we realized we could not outrun the threat or fight, the logical response was to freeze in the hope that the danger would not see us and would pass us by. This is how opossums defend themselves from predators. They play dead.

In modern organizations, fighting is usually unacceptable, and flight is equally unacceptable since we must stay on the job and get the work done. This leaves the third response of freezing. Most organizations are a collection of individuals freezing and hoping that the change passes them by. It's a game of "playing possum" organizationally, which might be the worst scenario.

Our observation is that it is amazingly easy for leaders to create this condition of inaction in their organization and not be aware of it. One CEO of a large regional bank was very excited to announce an upcoming merger. During an organization-wide communication meeting, explaining the rationale for the merger, the CEO said, "I know everyone's plate is full and that this merger is going to add a lot of additional work to everyone's load, but we are just going to push through it and get it done."

Observers could hear a collective sigh and feel the energy leave the virtual room. While this CEO had the best intentions and wanted to transfer his excitement to the rest of the organization, he inadvertently tripped the amygdalae of many in the meeting. It was as if he tripped a collective organizational amygdala.

All personal change is biological

We are thinking beings. We think all day and night, even as we sleep. A point that is often overlooked is that as we think, we *choose*. This choice sets in motion a chain of events that causes genetic expressions in your brain. This means the brain makes proteins, and these proteins form thoughts. From this perspective, thoughts are physical things that occupy space in the biological brain.

Eric R. Kandel, a Nobel Prize–winning neuroscientist, writes in his book *In Search of Memory* that even thoughts in our fabricated imaginations can turn on and off specific genes, thereby changing the structure of neurons in the brain.[9] So as we think and imagine, we change the design of the brain—moment to moment, our thinking and choosing redesigns neurons.[10]

The mind is designed to control the body, of which the brain is a part.

Fundamentally, we control matter through our thinking and choosing. As the ancient Stoic philosophers pointed out, we do not control the events but our reactions. When we are in control of our responses, we change our brains. It's not easy; it takes work. But it can be done through thoughts and choices. You are free to make choices about how you focus your attention. This affects how the chemicals, proteins, and wiring of your brain change and function.

As we've discussed before, neuroplasticity refers to the brain's ability to change and adapt both structurally and functionally in response to new experiences. Harvard Medical School's Alvaro Pascual-Leone states that neuroplasticity "is an intrinsic property of the human brain and represents evolution's invention to enable the nervous system to escape the restrictions of its own genome and thus adapt to environmental pressures, physiological changes, and experiences."[11]

Scientists now understand that the brain can be altered not only in childhood, but also throughout adulthood. Donald Hebb observed that "neurons that fire together, wire together." He was pointing out that the very basis of learning and change happens at the cellular level. In Hebb's book, *The Organization of Behavior*, he states, "When an axon of cell A is near enough to excite cell B and repeatedly or persistently takes part in firing it, some growth process or metabolic changes takes place in one or both cells."[12]

Considering the implications of neuroplasticity for leadership and culture, it becomes clear that all learning and change occur in the nervous system. This means the purpose of all training programs, town hall meetings, workshops, seminars, executive coaching, and team alignment sessions, whether we are aware of it, is to effect change in the brain and nervous system. Ignoring the importance of biology in the change process significantly limits our understanding of actual change.

Changing ineffective ways of thinking and ultimately behaving is a significant challenge. To make this change, we must learn both individually and collectively. But in considering the order of effect, it becomes clear that individual learning, personal change, and specifically change in the individual's mind must happen before collective learning and cultural change can happen.

It may seem strange to state that culture is a biological activity, but considering people are biological entities, the interaction between people is inevitably a biological endeavor.

The world as we know it only exists within our nervous system. We participate in the world through the nervous system. The nervous system's structure is the primary determinant of how any living entity responds to its environment. The nervous system can continually change.

Humberto Maturana, a Chilean biologist and philosopher, proposed an inside-out interpretation. What is perceived is more influenced by the nervous system's activity than what happens in the world. He suggests that we do not see things as they are. We see them according to how we are.[13]

Resistance to change is often a function of homeostasis, the natural movement of any organism toward equilibrium and away from change. But if we leverage the fact that the brain is a pattern-making organ with an innate desire to create novel connections, we can overcome this resistance.

Attention continually reshapes the patterns of the brain. By paying enough attention to anything, the brain keeps the pertinent circuits open and able to change. The circuits, over time, become not just temporary chemical links but physical changes in the brain's structure.

This is the power of focus. The brain changes as a function of where an individual puts their attention. This focus often challenges organizations as individuals in various units or functions to focus on different items and therefore think differently. These mental maps play a central role in perception.

Flavor of month (icing the puck)

One other barrier to change involves the concept of the "flavor of the month." This occurs when organizations introduce many change programs but rarely follow through with any of them. Generally, employees have learned that if they just wait long enough, another change program will take the place of the previous change program. This means that employees never have to change. They merely wait in place.

As we've already discussed, managers and leaders in organizations are dealing with a tremendous amount of change in the world around them. And trying to address these changes, they implement numerous change programs. While their intentions are good, the effect can be catastrophic.

This flavor of the month concept or phenomenon especially becomes insidious if we look at it from the perspective of neuroscience. As previously introduced, a mirror neuron fires when a person is watching the action of other people. In other words, the neuron "mirrors" the other person's action. As new programs are introduced in organizations, members watch what others around them do. Did they respond positively to the change? Do they resist the change? Do they simply ignore the change?

It is our observation that in many organizations, while individuals vocally support change efforts, their actions tell a different story. The action demonstrates, "I'm going to wait to see if this is a true change." This action then influences others in the organization through the mirror neurons. A network is created among organization members to resist the change.

In one sizable consulting firm, this activity of vocally supporting change efforts but behaviorally not supporting them was called "icing the puck." In hockey, if the defense sends the puck over the center line and it crosses the opposing goal line untouched and is then retrieved by an opposing player, icing is called. It is a delaying tactic used by the defense to change player lines and reposition the defense.

In organizations, teams often engage in delay tactics in the hope that leadership will lose focus on the current change initiative in favor of a new change initiative. The team's actions are rewarded because they can successfully defer the risk of taking any new action, and the desire to change passes by like a cloud in the sky.

In summary, change is driven by the hidden elements of culture, including social psychology and neuroscience. We need to tip the balance in favor of the desire to change over the fear of failure and acknowledge that personal change takes time to rewire the brain through successful repetitions of the new actions.

KEY TAKEAWAYS

- All culture and personal change is biological change. Unless neurons make new connections, changes in actions do not happen.
- As leaders, we can inadvertently trip the amygdalae of our teams (like a circuit breaker) and shut down their ability to reason, be curious, and exercise judgment.
- Change takes work and can cause discomfort if we focus only on the obvious elements of culture.
- Left unchecked, individuals, teams, and organizations tend to resist the change they desire and need.
- By better understanding how people learn and how the brain responds to change, leaders can facilitate change and create cultures that are more change-ready.

QUESTIONS TO CONSIDER

- What are some ways you unintentionally create learning anxiety in teams and the organization that are causing people to resist change?
- What are the typical states of mind you observe in your team? In the organization? How might those support or get in the way of the change you are trying to create?
- How have you created psychological safety and experiences that align teams to the ideal actions you need to get business results?
- What might we learn from mirror neurons and neuroplasticity to help you accelerate the transformation you want to see in the organization?
- How are you asking for and sharing feedback about individual and team performance? How are you gathering feedback from the organization about communicating and acting as a leader?

CHAPTER 8
HEALTHY WAYS TO OVERCOME RESISTANCE

> ***Every time you are tempted to react in the same old way, ask if you want to be a prisoner of the past or a pioneer of the future.***
>
> **DEEPAK CHOPRA**

Let's put this all together. How do we shape mindsets and thinking in the organization in a manner that does not trip the amygdala or create unnecessary work and discomfort for organizational members or allow "icing the puck"? In addition, how do we ensure the desire to change is more salient than the fear of screwing things up? We can take some simple actions to dramatically increase the positive transformational outcomes we seek.

As we have discussed, culture change requires a change in thinking, which is ultimately a change in the connections in the brain. Change in thinking implies that a new concept or thought has been introduced to an individual or group of individuals. Often these concepts are presented in the form of language. The key is to introduce concepts in a psychologically safe and neutral way. Our experience has guided us toward four levers to overcome resistance to change:

- Introduce intuitive and straight-forward concepts.
- Create healthy states of mind.
- Create a common experience to align teams.
- Leverage neuroscience to sustain ideal actions and better results.

INTRODUCE INTUITIVE AND STRAIGHTFORWARD CONCEPTS

First, it is critical to introduce concepts that are easy to understand and notice in ourselves and others. These concepts (as discussed in Chapter 6) are shortcuts to help us detect and choose the ideal actions necessary to get results. These also serve another critical purpose: they help decrease learning anxiety by introducing change in a way that is non-threatening. These concepts must be aligned with change, culture, and leadership principles. Often, we find that discussing the concepts is simple, but the application is not easy.

Edgar Schein pointed out that the key to changing culture—and maybe the key to *all* change—is establishing common concepts and a common language within an organization.[1] The reason this is important is so that we have a common basis for discussion and communication. To make a system-wide change, we must establish common concepts in a safe and neutral way.

This means we ask leaders and organization members to notice how certain concepts show up for them in their work life. The question then becomes, when is this working for you, and when is it working against you? Leaders then must be *deliberate, intentional,* and *purposeful* about change and what concepts they introduce. We've seen over and over in organizational psychology and cognitive psychology that the brain wants to focus on solutions instead of problems. It's more effective to create new thinking that will create new actions for the future.

The trick is less about the concepts and more about how the concepts are introduced. For concepts to be helpful, insights of individuals must be generated from within. As the adage says, "People will tolerate your conclusions, but act on their own." This means people must make their own conclusions instead of being given conclusions. This is best achieved using the Socratic method and experiential learning within intact work teams. That is solution-focused questioning that facilitates self-insight rather than telling or giving advice.

Also, as stated previously, people's neural networks are influenced by biology and attention. Brains are very complex. There is little point in trying to figure out how another person ought to reorganize their thinking. It is far more effective to help others come to their own insights about key concepts.

Once leaders create new insight, they can choose the amount of attention paid to specific mental experiences. The greater the concentration on a specific idea, the higher the attention density and the likelihood that the neurons wire together. This is known as *self-directed neuroplasticity*.

For leadership, the challenge is to give the right mental maps enough focus. Leaders must recognize that individual brains create new mental maps in real time. Leaders can make big differences in what they *model*, what they *reward*, and what they *tolerate* in the workplace to provide organization members with the needed level of focus.

DEVELOP HEALTHY STATES OF MIND

Second, when people are at their best (in a healthy state of mind), they tend to act in ways consistent with the concepts in the language we're establishing. When individuals are in an unhealthy state of mind, they tend to resort to automatic pilot and display unhealthy actions that undermine results.

Keeping actions simple and intuitive helps to overcome learning anxiety. In most cases, the concepts we need to be most effective are ones that most people already understand. We find they've simply forgotten them as they get busy with day-to-day work. Everyday stress can lead to an unhealthy state of mind that blocks us from clearly seeing our behaviors and the intuitive, effective actions needed to optimize performance.

Keeping things simple reduces learning anxiety and allows people to move through change while maintaining a healthy state of mind. And maintaining a healthy state of mind allows us to access the innate wisdom that will connect us deeply to all of the concepts and actions we need to produce results.

CREATE A COMMON EXPERIENCE TO ALIGN TEAMS

Third, once you create a set of concepts representing your ideal culture, you must create a shared experience to align teams to live the concepts consistently. This is the hidden aspect of cultural transformation that most organizations ignore. The concepts fade away without aligning teams to the language and breed cynicism.

How do you align teams? You need to have leaders operating from a healthy state of mind. This is another hidden element of culture that teams often ignore. They do offsites and align on the common concepts or exercises to help align the team, but teams are busy-minded from the day-to-day stress. They simply don't have the healthy perspective they need to consider a new way of working.

Within our process, we help leaders build trust, psychological safety, and a healthy state of mind *before* introducing concepts neutrally. This combination of healthy mind states with introducing concepts to allow people to be naturally curious dramatically improves the alignment process.

Once we have embedded some of the concepts into the working memory of the team, we allow the leaders more time to rewire their brains by reinforcing concepts and putting them into day-to-day work experiences. We often support this through direct coaching within meetings as well as training champions within teams to notice and guide the team to put these concepts to work. These champions often serve as role models, creating an ideal *reflection of leadership* for the team to mimic.

Finally, we help the team develop a healthy way to ask for and share feedback to reinforce the ideal actions. Over time, these new healthy habits are strengthened and become the accepted *way we do things around here.*

LEVERAGE NEUROSCIENCE TO SUSTAIN IDEAL ACTIONS AND BETTER RESULTS

The final step is to leverage *mirror neurons* and *neuroplasticity* to sustain the ideal actions over time. Just as mirror neurons have the potential to slow change, we can also use our understanding of the function of mirror neurons to accelerate change within teams. For example, the team's mirror neurons constantly scan to determine how to act. We can intentionally position culture champions to activate mirror neurons in this team by demonstrating the ideal actions and helping others feel safe behaving similarly. Subconsciously, the team begins to follow the champions' lead until, essentially, the whole team is acting as culture champions and creating a powerful *reflection of leadership* down through the organization.

To elicit sustainable change, we must support the rewiring of our brains through neuroplasticity. In essence, we need some old neural pathways to fade and new neural pathways to be strengthened. Through feedback and coaching, we can help both extinguish old actions and reinforce new ones to create new individual and collective autopilot actions aligned with the culture we want to create.

KEY TAKEAWAYS

- While the need for change is constant, change takes work and can cause discomfort if the only focus is the obvious elements of culture.
- There are four levers to overcome resistance to change: intuitive and straight-forward concepts, healthy states of mind, aligned teams, and neuroscience.
- Culture transformation leverages neuroscience to transform the *thinking* of human beings to align with new ways of *doing* things.
- Common concepts and language are shortcuts to healthy states of mind as well as clear communications about the preferred way of acting.
- Once preferred concepts and language are defined, intact teams need experiences that allow them to engage with the concepts and begin to shift their thinking.
- When people are at their best, they can more easily act consistent with concepts and language.
- To drive culture transformation, keep things *simple* and *intuitive* to reduce learning anxiety.

QUESTIONS TO CONSIDER

- What are some points of resistance to change within your organization?
- Have you distilled the critical symbols and language that will guide the culture and accelerate the business strategy?
- How have you aligned intact teams to behave in alignment with the cultural symbols and language?
- How do the interventions leverage neuroscience, including mirror neurons, the amygdala trip, and neuroplasticity?

- What actions are you taking to maintain healthy states of mind in your organization to reduce resistance to change and align thinking and behaviors to your ideal culture?

CHAPTER 9
THE HIDDEN ROLE OF THOUGHT IN YOUR CULTURE

There are no facts, only interpretations.

FRIEDRICH NIETZSCHE

As we move in and out of organizations to help assess and transform cultures, it is easy for *us* to see the water people are swimming in (even though it is often hidden for clients). We can see the shared experiences that have led to accepted beliefs and ways of operating. We can also quickly notice the typical states of mind that people tend to experience. And yet, early on in our work with clients, most leaders seem to be gripped by how they see the culture—mistaking it for reality.

GETTING GRIPPED BY THE MOVIE

Recall a trip to a movie that was a thriller, packed full of action. Most likely, you were gripped by the movie at times. You likely had physiological reactions: sweaty palms, ducking your head to dodge obstacles, flinching from punches from another actor, or even an elevated heart rate and blood pressure. Why did you experience these physiological changes when watching photons (perceived as scenes) on a screen and experiencing pressure waves (perceived as sounds) in a theater? It's because the movie gripped you.

You no doubt realized that it was just a movie. You broadened your perspective beyond the boundaries of the screen, and you remembered that you were in a movie theater. You also realized that the lead actor (who was paid millions to star in the movie) probably didn't die in the first fifteen minutes. As your body relaxed, you also noticed there were others around you in the movie theater and some were gripped as you just were; others may not have been gripped. Some were not even paying attention to the screen; perhaps they were looking at their phones, or even sleeping. And, your perspective suddenly changed. You could see the bigger picture and *notice yourself and others as shown in Figure 9.1*.

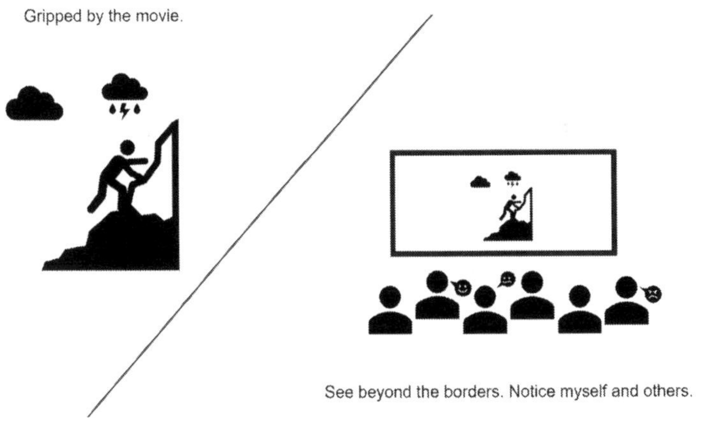

Figure 9.1 How life appears when you are gripped by a movie and when you can see beyond the borders of the screen—noticing yourself and others.

Just as we can be gripped by a movie, we are often gripped by experiences at work. For example, recall a tense meeting from the past. Perhaps, your organization missed a critical goal, and you needed to figure out what went wrong and fix it. How quickly were you *gripped* by the meeting? You might have experienced tension in your shoulders, an elevated heart rate, and even sweaty palms as you listened to someone blaming you or your team for what went wrong. Your thinking (based on past experiences) was filling in the story, much as the Hollywood special effects crew created the movie elements that gripped you in the theater and triggered your physiological responses.

When a meeting grips us, we are in an unhealthy state of mind. Our amygdala mistakes the psychological fear we experience for physical fear that it protected us from for millennia. Precious oxygen is diverted to our large muscle groups to get us ready for fight or flight, and then the prefrontal cortex that allows us to reason and exercise judgment is starved of oxygen. We lean in and fight, or we withdraw. As the meeting continues, results are elusive, and relationships can be damaged.

And, yet there is another way to experience the meeting—just as there was another way to experience the movie. We can broaden our perspective and see beyond what is being said. We can see that the meeting grips many, but some are checked out. We can also see that we are filling in the experience with our built-in "special effects crew" to elevate the drama and increase our physiological response. That's what is really happening. And, when we realize what's happening, our perspective returns, and our amygdala restores oxygen to our prefrontal cortex and elevates our wisdom, judgment, and reasoning. This is the state of mind that is critical to recovering from a setback in the business.

We often encounter teams gripped by their experiences. For instance, we once worked with an executive team facing disappointing financial results during the current quarter. The perspective gripped team members that being a publicly traded company unfairly put them on a treadmill of quarterly results expectations from investors. They feared that if they stepped off the treadmill's steady pace by missing even one quarter of earnings, their stock would be negatively impacted. The team felt they couldn't afford to make the real investments needed to grow the business because that would cause them to miss a quarter's earnings expectation. The executive team was gripped by the "publicly traded treadmill" movie. It existed in their collective minds as if it were reality. And, it was creating an unhealthy state of mind—that was getting in the way of making progress against the current and future quarters.

So, we asked, "How else would you like to fund the company?" After a brief pause and a couple of clarifying questions, they began to explore a broader set of options. Have you considered private equity? "We'd lose control over everything. They'd want to change how we operate. And, they have even higher expectations of returns than our board and shareholders do." Would you like to fund the company yourselves? "We can't—don't have that kind of money." Want to sell your company to a larger competitor? "Hell no."

Once we could step back and help them see the *movie* they were accepting as reality, they gained perspective and were able to return to a healthy state of mind and move forward, exploring how this team could have an even greater impact on results.

SEPARATE REALITIES

Because we each have our own unique filters that impact how we perceive the world around us, we essentially experience separate realities. For example, have you ever left a movie and turned to your friend to share how much you liked the movie, only to find out that they hated it? You may also find that some of your friends identified or defended characters that others were attacking. The truth is that we all interpret the world around us through our senses and filters. We *experience separate realities*—even when we go to the same movie.

Our minds fill in gaps and omit things, even when we are in the same movie or attend the same meeting at work. It is an *illusion* that we experience the same reality. For example, have you ever experienced a meeting where you felt the team was aligned on what to do next, only to find out that people moved in different directions? How can this be? We were crystal clear about what we needed to do next! Let's explore this idea of being crystal clear in our communications.

The assumption of being crystal clear is to assume that we experience the external world the same way. But, our sensory organs act as interpreters, experiencing millions of photons of light (sights), air compression waves (sounds), molecular structures (smells, tastes), textures (touch), and temperatures (touch). We then *individually* translate those into electrochemical signals in *each* of our brains and rely on those unique signals to make sense of the world.[1]

For example, in the physical world, there is no such thing as *color*. Our eyes are tuned to sense a tiny band of wavelengths of energy, and our visual cortex translates these wavelengths into distinct colors. Color exists in our brain, not out in the world. Dogs, for example, don't see colors. They see mostly shades of gray. Even some humans are color blind, not seeing the same colors that others may see.

The illusion of a shared reality doesn't just happen at the individual level. These illusions can also happen in teams and in the organization as a whole. We often experience the grips of an *accepted shared external reality* in organizations as we move from client to client. Accepting these shared understandings as external reality can become limiting beliefs that prevent us from achieving results:

- "We are a publicly traded company, so we have to stay on the treadmill of consistent and predictable earnings" (preventing us from making the necessary investment to outgrow our competitors).
- "We have to innovate even though it strains relationships with customers and associates" (preventing us from providing the next level of service expected by customers).
- "We don't like being owned by one of the largest companies in the world" (preventing us from optimizing the division as part of the whole and learning from the rest of the organization).
- "Since we're privately funded, we don't have the money to invest in developing leaders" (leading to increased turnover and stagnation of results).
- "We're the largest organization in our industry, so we can't be agile" (allowing competitors to outflank and steal market share).
- "We're the world's first organization and oldest in this industry" (leading to complacency and being outpaced by faster-growing startups).
- "Our culture is pretty good, at least compared to industry benchmarks" (preventing an organization from creating an economic advantage through culture).

These shared and accepted "realities" become limiting beliefs and thought habits in organizational cultures. And, when newcomers test them, existing employees are quick to become gripped by someone challenging what they know is an "objective" reality. This dysfunction plays out in every organization.

HOW UNDERSTANDING THE ROLE OF THOUGHT CAN HELP YOU TRANSFORM YOUR CULTURE

Recognizing the role of thought helps us elevate our thinking and gain perspective. Perspective lets us notice when we accept limiting beliefs, allow ourselves to be gripped by meetings, experience a healthier state of mind more often, and choose the actions that will optimize our business. In essence, recognizing our thinking creates a healthier state of mind, which is the precursor to a healthy culture.

So, how do we get to a healthy state of mind more often and more quickly? We have to quiet our busy minds.

Thoughts are the precursors to state of mind

Feeling at your best or off your game is analogous to being in a healthy or unhealthy state of mind. For example, grateful thoughts create grateful states of mind. In contrast, worried thoughts create anxious states of mind. As human beings, we have up to 70,000 thoughts going through our heads daily. Many of these thoughts are recycled, showing up repeatedly throughout each day or even each hour.

These thoughts tend to bubble up in our minds like a popcorn machine. "Leah is going to hate this report. She has very high expectations. She is always critical of our reports, and I'm not good at reports. She went to an Ivy League school, and I didn't. I'm not a great writer."

Imagine seeing all of these thoughts popping up. And some tend to show up over and over again. Subconsciously, we begin to program our brains to generate *feelings* of insecurity, worry, anxiety, or self-doubt. These *feelings* are a guide to the quality of our *thinking*.

More often, we are unaware of our unconscious minds' underlying thoughts. They simply flow through us as water flows through a riverbed. We can't always notice our thinking, but we can easily notice the feelings that result from our thinking. And, knowing that thinking drives our state of mind, we can estimate the quality of our thinking. If we feel an unhealthy state of mind, like insecurity—we have unreliable thinking. If we feel a higher state of mind, like confidence, we can trust our thinking.

Sometimes, we can slow down our busy minds and start noticing some underlying thoughts creating these states of mind. For example, not getting an immediate and positive response to a sales proposal can sometimes trigger insecurity. "We're not good at sales. The proposal wasn't as good as it should have been. Maybe we didn't listen as well as we should have. Did we not even establish the need or share the value of our work?" And, if we don't notice them, they operate as *hidden,* and we don't understand why we feel off our game.

In Figure 9.2, we describe what we call the Thought Cycle. Thinking—either conscious or unconscious—creates a higher or lower state of mind, which in turn influences our actions that generate results. Notice that this cycle is iterative. One positive turn can generate positive results for us to notice and think about, spiraling upward. The converse can also be true, causing us to spiral downward and become less and less effective.

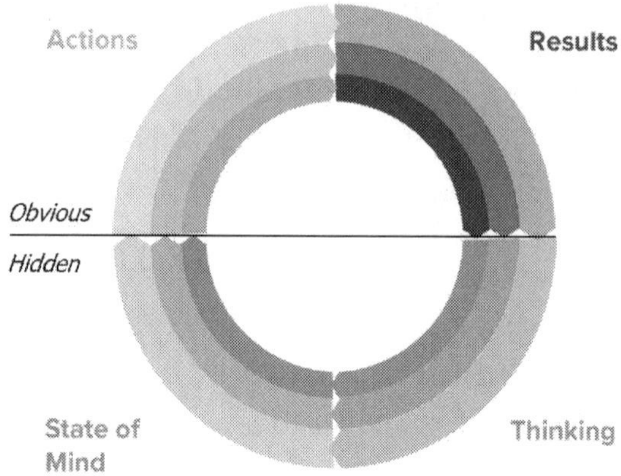

Figure 9.2 The Thought Cycle.

Our day-to-day experience with life isn't created for us. We create our experiences starting with our thinking. With practice, we can more quickly notice our thinking and shift it. With the shift in thinking, we can generate better odds at spending time at our best—in healthy states of mind. Even small shifts in these odds are remarkably different for those around us.

The key to noticing and shifting our thinking is to *quiet our minds.*

Learning to be quiet-minded

Each of us has experienced a *busy mind.* While speaking with someone, our thoughts drift, turning to what's next, what we experienced before the conversation, how we are looking, and whether this is worth continuing. It's natural for us to experience this busy mind, but it isn't a healthy state. The more time we can spend with quieter minds, the better we are at leading with empathy, building trust, driving results, and living in a higher state of mind.

There are many benefits to spending more time being quiet-minded. For millennia, we have learned about the value of quieting our minds. In addition to helping us be ready to better interact with each other, there are many health benefits from being still and silent, such as:[2]

- Lower blood pressure
- Decreased heart rate
- Bring breathing under control
- Reduced muscle tension
- Reduced risk of heart attack
- Increased focus and cognition
- Increased life expectancy

With regard to increasing life expectancy, Elizabeth Blackburn won a Nobel Prize in 2009 for showing that meditation increases the length of telomeres, which are the end of our chromosomes.[3] Longer telomeres have been shown to predict a longer natural life span.

The reasons above should be enough to convince you that quieting your mind is important, but there is also a profound need related to shaping organizational culture. *Culture* essentially *lives in our minds*. By that, we mean that the thought habits, beliefs, and ways we expect to relate to each other are all sitting in our brains, typically hidden in our subconscious minds. The only way to begin to see these hidden thought habits and beliefs is to *quiet our minds so we can notice them and choose better alternatives*.

We were working with a CEO of a large, global consumer products company and this notion of quieting his mind took him. An Ivy League graduate, he had always struggled with being busy-minded, so much so that he committed to spending more time in a quiet mind. To help him better understand how to quiet his mind after our session, he purchased approximately twelve books on reflection, meditation, and so forth that he showed me during our next coaching session. I paused, sensing some humor in the moment, and suggested that this could turn into a perfect irony—six months of coaching, dozens of books, and still a busy mind. He agreed and turned to meditation instead.

How to quiet your mind

How you quiet your mind is up to you. Some use smartphone apps for guided meditation, others practice yoga, and others use exercise to let go of their busy minds. We have found that it can be as simple as taking a few deep breaths. As a matter of fact, do that now:

- Inhale slowly and deeply through your nose.
- Breathe out through your mouth and pause for a few seconds.
- Inhale again slowly through your nose.
- Then, breathe out one more through your mouth and pause.

How do you feel? If you are like many of our clients, you simply forget to do such simple things throughout your busy day.

Being quiet-minded takes you off autopilot and accelerates culture transformation

Quieting your mind not only helps you be healthier, it also turns off your autopilot. Change can only take place if you take yourself off autopilot.

To shift our thinking and behaviors, we have to *notice* them. We cannot notice them with a busy mind—only with a quiet mind. Once we have quieted our minds, we can *notice* our thinking and behaviors and *choose* the ones we want. That's the most fundamental process to personal, team, and organizational change—the ability to notice your thinking, state of mind, or behaviors and choose a different option.

There is tremendous power in slowing down the mind to reflect on how we feel and noticing how we behave and what those around us are experiencing. Only then can we resurface those habits dwelling in our subconscious and commit to making small shifts in those habits to create a better culture at work.

One of our favorite CEOs went through an offsite experience to slow down his thinking and notice some of his autopilot tendencies. Of course, many of his learned behaviors were serving him and the organization remarkably well. They had recovered from a downward trend in revenue with negative EBITDA to an organization that was growing revenue and building significant EBITDA.

However, he realized he was doing a few things that didn't serve the team or the organization as well as he would have liked. As a *confident vulnerable* leader, he captured the areas he wanted to develop in his journal, then had them blown up poster-sized, hung them on his office door, and signed them. This CEO set a powerful example for the organization by using confident vulnerability to build followers.

HEALTHY STATES OF MIND UNLEASH ACCOUNTABILITY

We were once working with the North American division of a global consumer company. This division had been working to develop a culture of accountability for over five years, requiring every employee to go through a two-day accountability learning experience as part of their onboarding. And yet, as we completed our culture assessment, accountability was one of their lowest scores.

As we were working with the leadership team, we noticed that discussing accountability became heated, and, very quickly, the team moved to a defensive and unhealthy state of mind. This caused them to be gripped by the movie of poor business results and eventual layoffs that tended to come in the late fall to achieve the EPS targets they committed to the street.

We took a quick break and came back in with an exercise that helped them gain perspective and a healthier state of mind. Then we helped them explore how accountability *felt different* from a healthy state of mind. Like a light bulb, one of the leaders jumped up and took a picture of the slide we were sharing and said, "That's it! We have to develop healthy states of mind to get accountable leaders!"

You can quickly be gripped by the movie while driving culture transformation. You won't notice it in yourself or others. Just as you start to feel the intensity of the movie, use our three-step process for driving deliberate, intentional, and purposeful cultures:

- Quiet your mind.
- Notice yourself and others.
- Choose actions that will create the culture you really want.

KEY TAKEAWAYS

- We can be gripped by our experience at work the same way we are gripped by watching a movie, causing us to lose perspective and effectiveness.
- No two thought systems are the same—we see separate realities even when we have shared experiences.
- We experience two states of mind at work (and at home): healthy (at our best) and unhealthy (off our game).
- The Thought Cycle helps us notice that our thinking creates our state of mind that influences our actions and creates our results.
- Be quiet-minded—quiet your mind, notice yourself and others, and choose the actions that will create the culture you want and deliver results.

QUESTIONS TO CONSIDER

- As you experience meetings at work, what do you notice about your state of mind and those of your team members? How might that be accelerating or impeding your results?
- What are the experiences at work that seem to grip you, limiting your ability to be at your best?
- What have you found to be effective ways to quiet your mind?
- Does your organization offer support for being more mindful at work?
- What shared thinking that has become accepted by your organization is really just limiting beliefs that prevent you from succeeding?

CHAPTER 10
CONFIDENT VULNERABILITY, THE WAY OF BEING

There are three things that are extremely hard: steel, a diamond, and to know one's self.

BENJAMIN FRANKLIN

We just reviewed the power of a quiet mind and healthy states of mind in creating a healthy culture. In addition to the principles and mechanics of systematically transforming cultures, it is important to consider a foundational condition that can dramatically improve your ability to transform your culture: being confident, vulnerable leaders successfully. In our experience, leaders must also be able, willing, and public about their capacity for growth and learning.

Why is confident vulnerability so important? Because confident and vulnerable leaders have a healthy state of mind, they notice their actions and choose ideal ones. Leaders who feel insecure (as we all do, from time to time) will have unhealthy states of mind that tend to block their ability even to notice their actions. They go on autopilot and let the subconscious mind take over—doing what has always made sense to them without consciously thinking about it.

Leaders who lack the ability to access their own vulnerability tend to feel they have no blind spots, growth opportunities, or new things to learn. Without the confidence to be vulnerable, we lack the capacity for personal change. More importantly, the leader's reflection influences the broader organization. Through the mirror neurons of others, we block personal change in those in our teams and throughout the organization. This lack of *confident vulnerability* is a hidden aspect of culture transformation and the *number one reason* we see culture transformation efforts stall or fail.

In fact, confident vulnerability is the one element we look for in leaders and leadership teams, or at least we look for the ability and willingness to develop confident vulnerability as a predictor of our success. If we see confident vulnerability in action in the leader or leadership team, we know our method of transformation will work. On the other hand, when this element is not demonstrated or the desire to develop it is blocked, we have experienced that change is hard and takes a lot of work. In fact we are reminded of Sisyphus, in Greek mythology, who was fated by Zeus, for eternity, to roll a huge rock up one side of a hill, only to watch it roll down the other side when he got to the top. Then he would start over. That's what change feels like in organizations with lower levels of confident vulnerability. Leaders are not clear and confident in their direction and are not humble, open, and curious enough to find new and better ways. We believe this is why so much frustration, cynicism, and dissatisfaction exist in most organizations today.

HOW DOES USING AUTOPILOT BEHAVIORS CREATE CULTURES?

Just as we first learned to ride a bike or drive a car, we also needed to first learn how to do certain tasks at work: procedures, communicating with team members, managing others, rewarding performance, turning around a company, and creating healthy cultures. And, just as with riding a bike or driving a car, we tend to offload most of these learned behaviors to our subconscious mind, allowing it to run the show.

As reviewed earlier, in the process of learning, the brain tends to push deliberate thinking into the subconscious areas of the brain. Maintaining your balance, scanning the road ahead, and watching for obstacles benefit from the processing power of the subconscious mind. They became *automatic*. Bike riding was moved to the subconscious mind where it can be stored in the structures of your brain for the long term. In essence, it became a form of autopilot. You just know how to do it. Even if you haven't ridden a bike for decades, you can just get on and ride because it is permanently wired into your subconscious (unconscious) mind and it operates even though you don't think about it.

Think about it: Do you start meetings right on time or 10 minutes past? Do you ask for everyone's point of view before making a decision, or do you listen to the leader of that area? Do you encourage your team to take risks or reward them for reducing risk? Do you reward firefighting by those who created the fires or those who have no fire to fight because they prevented it in the first place? What is your leadership autopilot?

Over the years, we offload most everything to the vast and capable subconscious mind, including most of how we act as we work together in organizations. The subconscious becomes the source for everything that is effective (and less effective) in working with others. It is our source of belief that we can achieve most anything as well as the root of our limiting beliefs that can hold us back.

As we live our lives, we often rely on autopilot without careful consideration of what we programmed into autopilot in the first place. We may have seen someone get promoted by acting in their self-interest versus the interest of the larger team or organization, which became our default way of operating. We may have had a person we respect tell us that we can't do something, and we begin to believe it, developing a limiting belief about what is possible.

When our autopilot seems to be *working* for us, we feel little need to examine it through our consciousness. We just let it run and we learn to trust it. However, as conditions change in the markets or within your organization, some of our actions are no longer as effective. As performance requirements change, some subconscious habits can often *get in the way* of results. This same phenomenon which plays out at the individual level also exists at the collective team, and organization levels.

For example, as we work with large financial institutions, they built such a strong risk aversion mindset stemming from the Great Recession of 2008, that they struggle to grow their businesses and compete with fintech startups who never developed that risk aversion mindset in the first place.

The CEO's number one priority was innovation to grow the business. Yet, the risk-adverse mindsets embedded in the organization, and especially in the leader ranks, squelched almost all innovative thinking. This leadership team was very good at shooting down ideas. As one executive recounted, "Now I see there is an element of risk in all change. I thought, don't let people go down rabbit holes and waste time on things we have already tried. This is wasteful and risky. Now I understand that I will get no new ideas unless I can be curious about new ideas and help people develop them. I now see my job is to encourage new thinking and to protect the organization from unnecessary risk through active engagement. It's not an either-or."

This is *confident vulnerability* in action—to be humble and curious about new ideas, which may threaten current ways of doing things, and the courage and confidence to know that we will move ahead appropriately and achieve results.

These autopilot habits can also be more subtle. As two companies begin to integrate (through a merger or acquisition), leaders can feel enormous barriers between how "we" and "they" operate when culture diagnostics show that the companies are similar in almost every aspect.

In a merger of two energy companies, we found the two companies were parallel on nearly every common culture dimension (integrity, collaboration, accountability, etc.). But as we worked with the companies, it was clear that each company's thinking about budgets was very different. One company viewed budgets as a "general" guidepost and made exceptions liberally to gain market share. The second company regarded budgets as absolute and made no exceptions. Leaders were expected to manage precisely to their budget. The two companies were essentially operating on two different budget autopilots, resulting in a lot of unnecessary tension and conflict, especially during integration meetings. Once we were able to raise these basic assumptions to awareness, they could address the difference constructively. Moving these thought habits to a conscious level allows us to examine our autopilots and to choose deliberate, intentional, and purposeful actions to meet the current business demands.

CONFIDENT VULNERABILITY HELPS YOU NOTICE AND RESHAPE AUTOPILOT HABITS AND, THEREFORE, CULTURE

Psychiatrist Carl Jung observed, "Until you make the unconscious conscious, it will direct your life, and you will call it fate." Exploring this often-hidden part of who you are is the precursor to personal change, and thus all culture change.

To best understand the importance of leaders displaying confident vulnerability and being open to exploring what may be hidden in their unconscious minds—accumulated over entire careers—we will share an encounter with a CEO of a large global consumer organization as we launched a culture transformation. To preserve confidentiality, we will use the name "Bill" for the CEO.

Late one winter, after being endorsed by the CHRO, we were introduced to Bill to gain his alignment on our approach to culture transformation. We entered his office and sat across from him at his large conference room table. The office was generously sized and included all sorts of awards and memorabilia. As we begin culture transformation, we start at the top—at least the top of a function or division. We do this to ensure that the reflection these leaders are casting into the organization aligns with the ideal culture.

We knew that Bill had been in the role for a little over five years and that he had previously been the CEO of a mid-sized consumer company that had been taken public (and rewarded him handsomely). He was a very confident and capable leader. He knew the industry and the products and was very familiar with a P&L and how to refine it. Given his capabilities, he often made decisions within the executive team.

For the first few minutes of our conversation, he relayed to us that his team was not very accountable. They waited for him to make all the decisions and were not proactive. He identified this as a barrier to their team culture and observed this behavior deeper in the organization. The lack of accountability was causing them to underperform as an organization and losing share in a few markets that were their core areas of strength.

To determine what may have caused this to become an operating norm within the team, we began asking questions about the *art* and *science* of the culture—exploring first the obvious elements, then attempting to uncover some hidden ones.

"Can you share an example?" we asked.

"Well, take last fall, for example. We were not going to make our numbers during the holiday season, and the team was willing to accept that and retreat to their vacations with their families," Bill said. "I was the one that insisted we not accept defeat, and I made the critical adjustments necessary to bring us over the finish line."

Becoming visibly irritated by reliving the story as he conveyed it, Bill concluded, "I have no idea why this team is so unaccountable for results when they are all so highly compensated!"

This was our first clue that something hidden from him was driving his team and, ultimately, his organizational culture. To help illuminate what was hidden, we asked what we thought would be a logical question, hoping to help him see what might be operating to create this norm: "Who on the team is most accountable, most often?" To that, he replied: "None of them."

Staying curious, we dug deeper. "Who on the team did you inherit versus hiring yourself?" (We asked this, even though we knew the answer from our preparation but thought it might help him start to piece this together.)

"I hired almost all of them myself," he replied.

So, we asked, "How long have they been working for you?"

He replied, "Most for three to five years. Some a little longer."

We took a bit of a bold step to help him see what was hidden and asked: "So, you hired most of the team. They have worked for you for more than three years. None of them are accountable, and you would like us to help improve that?"

"Yes!" he exclaimed, feeling we finally got what he was saying.

This leader was not demonstrating confident vulnerability, but rather insecure judgment and the feeling that he had it all figured out while everyone else was wrong. He was so caught up in his thinking that he could not even see his role in creating the same problems that he was criticizing. In fact, he was the one who had hired and led for years all of the people he believed were not performing.

CONFIDENT VULNERABILITY CREATES THE CAPACITY TO GROW AND CHANGE

One of the things we believe in doing this work is what Albert Einstein once famously shared: "No problem can be solved from the same consciousness that created it. We have to learn to see the world anew." At this time, and in Bill's current state of mind, he could not see what was hidden in the culture of his team. He could also not see how he might be contributing to it because his thinking was still at a lower level of consciousness.

We continued, "You know, Bill, to lead cultural transformation, it will be critical for you to look for and explore your role in creating this culture of low accountability."

"What?" he asked.

We clarified, "We are not saying that you are not accountable, nor that you are intentionally creating this operating norm, but to hire most of the team and have them all work for you for more than three years and for none of them to be accountable, will you at least stay curious to see what signals they may be getting from you that certain unaccountable actions are tolerated?"

Imagine yourself as a member of that senior executive team. Would you be ready to examine yourself and explore how you can be more effective?

To shape organizational culture, you must begin by helping your leaders rewire their brains. This action will assist them in eliminating unproductive habits and then replacing them with productive habits. One key strategy to accomplish this goal is to first assist them in becoming more conscious of their unproductive habits.

Next, they need to understand *why* they behave the way they do. Only then can they *choose* the behaviors they so deeply need to be effective in shaping or reshaping your culture. However, unless your leaders are open to beginning to make small changes in how they operate, no one else in your organization will think that it is safe for them to change.

A CEO DEMONSTRATES THE POWER OF CONFIDENT VULNERABILITY

To contrast our experience with Bill, we'll describe a different experience with a CEO whom we helped launch a global culture transformation at a global retailer. We will call this CEO Brandon to preserve his confidentiality.

Brandon was a Fortune 500 CEO at the time of the culture transformation we worked with him. He began his career with nothing, fresh out of business school. However, over the years, he accumulated several billion dollars net worth. After completing a culture alignment experience, Brandon had an epiphany that led to his kicking off an initiative focused on confident vulnerability with tremendous energy.

Brandon shared with his leadership team during our work with his organization, "We are starting at the top of the organization because I can't expect you to change if I don't. I learned something important about myself during this experience as I relayed my conversation with the investors to the team last month."

He continued, "I told them that we didn't make our revenue projection for the quarter due to uncooperative weather." (In this case, they sold clothing, and having a sharp change to the season tends to drive sales.) Brandon then shared, "By the end of the experience, I realized that all of my competitors had the same weather."

You could have heard a pin drop. This incredibly accomplished and confident CEO had suddenly shared that he was also, at times, not as accountable as he should be. While still confident, he was open and vulnerable.

Now, place yourself on his team—how excited would you be to explore areas for your personal growth after hearing from him? How safe would you feel exploring those areas under his leadership?

CONFIDENT VULNERABILITY ACCELERATES CULTURAL TRANSFORMATION

A longitudinal study, employing both interviews and statistical analysis, including over 90 regression analyses of thousands of executives, attempted to find the "best of the best executives."[1] A key finding of the study was that the best "form deep, trusting relationships." The best also led with "humble confidence that graciously extended care to others." This single dimension separates the best from the others and is a key ingredient in what we call *confident vulnerability.*

Let's unpack *confident vulnerability* and its critical role in driving cultural transformation. What we mean by *confident vulnerability* is that you realize, most importantly, you are willing to make mistakes and even fail. But from there, you learn and grow in the presence of others. We share as we learn new things from our errors or are surprised. As we make mistakes, we are comfortable sharing what we did and what we learned from it.

We share as we learn new things from our errors or are surprised.

For decades, CEO Boyd Clarke often closed meetings in Tom Peters's organization by saying, "Let's go out and learn something today." That simple statement set a clear and powerful message: we all *can* and *should* be learning something new daily.

While much has been written about effectiveness and vulnerability over the last ten years by various best-selling authors and experts (e.g., Brené Brown), we find that in most business instances, rightly or wrongly, the word *vulnerability* is often equated to failure. As such, this tends to trip the amygdala that we discussed earlier in leaders, triggering unhealthy states of mind and blocking the ability to consider the concept authentically.

In our experience, vulnerability is important but incomplete. We have observed that confidence is as essential as vulnerability. In many organizations, we witness leaders who share mea culpa after mea culpa, which encourages their teams to lose confidence in them. This often comes from an insecure mind and will not inspire others to follow you. They may begin to question your leadership increasingly. The lesson here? Having vulnerability without confidence is as ineffective at motivating people to change as confidence without vulnerability.

Confidence is about *accepting* and *trusting* yourself. It's also about having positive feelings about yourself and keeping a perspective as to what you do well (most things, most of the time) and what you could do even better (a few things, on occasion). Confidence is not about thinking you are perfect. It is also not about thinking that you don't make mistakes. It is about being comfortable with who you are, accepting yourself, and staying committed to the journey of ongoing learning and improvement.

There is a powerful, almost superpower effect in combining confidence with vulnerability. In this case, you are confident as a leader. You often perform very well—at your best. And yet, there are times when you make mistakes. There are times when you don't know. This realization of your vulnerabilities communicates a powerful message to those around you, "I am not perfect. I am here to learn and grow. And I will see the job through." Through this openness, others will share and learn from you vicariously and then get better. This approach builds trust in teams and allows them to truly work together.

Confident vulnerability is less of a characteristic or set of behaviors that can be learned and more of a natural way of being and mindset that permeates all actions. There is no training program, three key behaviors, or four steps to confident vulnerability. Instead, confident vulnerability is waiting to be discovered, and it's available to all of us at any time.

HOW DO YOU KNOW WHEN YOU ARE CONFIDENT AND VULNERABLE? IT'S ALL IN YOUR STATE OF MIND

There are times you may quickly recall from your life when you felt confident vulnerability. How would you know? You were self-assured in what you were doing and *comfortable* sharing your shortcomings. The humility of confident vulnerability, allows leaders to admit mistakes, own them, and work to overcome them through growth and learning. This superpower comes from being *at your best.* We call this a confident *state of mind,* which reflects a person's emotions, feelings, moods, and the effect these have on the person's thinking and actions and, ultimately, their effectiveness.

Let's explore this concept of being *at your best* as a *hidden* component of the *art of culture.* As you may have noticed, there are times you feel at your best and then there are other times that you feel off your game. As Figure 10.1 shows, state of mind is binary: healthy or unhealthy. It's like two sides of the same coin, two sides of yourself.

Figure 10.1 Your state of mind is either *unhealthy* or *healthy.*

When you are *at your best,* you feel like things come easily. We know we are at our best when we feel a sense of *confidence,* creativity, curiosity, optimism, and resilience. What are some of your feelings when you are at your best?

Whatever your list, you will feel prepared for any challenge you face. Your thinking at this time is reliable and you are fully available to partner effectively with others in the organization, be creative, and take ownership.

What's important to notice is your feelings, not the words that come to mind. Your feelings are always accurate, and you can notice them, even when you can't notice the subconscious thinking creating the feelings. In the most general terms, when you *feel confident,* you are at your best, and when you *feel insecure,* you are off your game. This is important to notice because you lose certain abilities when you are off your game.

Using your feelings as your guide can help explain many common organizational dysfunctions. For example, much of the conflict in organizations is rooted in individuals with unhealthy states of mind, including insecurity, frustration, anxiety, and anger. Why did it seem so important for you to argue one day, and the next, when you are in a healthier state of mind, you wonder why you even had the argument? How many times have you sent an email from an unhealthy state of mind and wished you could recall it? How many times have you come into work on the day after a very tough meeting with a colleague, after some rest and rejuvenation, only to see things differently and with more of an open mind?

We find leaders carrying narratives from years or even a decade ago around in their thinking. Well, you should have seen what that reorg did to our talent. When did it happen? About eight years ago—and we kept it alive, assigned it meaning and value, and let it push us into unhealthy states of mind: straining our relationships and blocking us from moving on productively with our work and lives.

Healthy states of mind form the basis of confident vulnerability. Unhealthy conditions of mind create dysfunction and barriers to effectiveness. Test this in your mind's eye. Have you ever had to deal with a tough issue while in an unhealthy state of mind? How did that work out?

In contrast, have you ever dealt with a challenging problem while in a state of confident vulnerability? How did that work out? Our experience has been that when leaders are in healthy states of mind and operate from a place of confident vulnerability, they can find solutions to even the toughest problems.

HOW CAN WE SPEND MORE TIME IN A HEALTHY STATE OF MIND TO BE CONFIDENTLY VULNERABLE?

It's perfectly natural for us to spend periods of our lives, days, and moments moving between unhealthy and healthy states of mind. Since we are human beings, we are not looking for perfection. We're simply looking to improve our balance of time in a healthy state of mind and operating from a place of confident vulnerability.

In working with leaders for several years, we have observed three consistently effective practices that aid in moving from unhealthy to healthier states of mind. The first is the ability and habit of quieting our busy minds. As we learned in previous chapters, this is a very powerful practice. A quiet mind can work through emotions effectively, notice what is happening around us, and see past mental frames and filters that often cloud our perspective.

The second practice is to be open and curious. Asking questions like, "What's truly going on here? I wonder how that makes sense to them? What am I missing?" and many others engage the brain. When the brain is engaged with a problem, neurotransmitters like dopamine, serotonin, and hormones like adrenaline are released into the body. This often provides a positive boost to mood states.

The third practice is gratitude. When people are in a grateful state, dopamine and serotonin are released into the body. While there is plenty of research about this, try a simple personal experiment. Stay in an unhealthy state of mind while expressing sincere gratitude about something or someone. See what happens.

One leadership team we worked with made a commitment to journal three things they were personally grateful for before entering the office building in the morning. These were personal journals so no one was required to share their thoughts. The team noticed and experienced healthier individual states of mind and a healthier "team" state of mind. This team state of mind created a tone of confident vulnerability, which exuded from the team and cascaded through the entire organization.

In working with this team, what we experienced and what we heard in gathering feedback from organizational members was a deep sense of authenticity. This authenticity stemmed from the confident vulnerability of the individual leaders and the collective leadership team. Confidence paired with vulnerability made these leaders authentic, and everyone felt it. Authenticity leads to greater trust in the organization because there are no games or hidden agendas. Trust sets the foundation for greater collaboration. Collaboration leads to teamwork. Teamwork unlocks the potential in the organization and unleashes the ability to deliver and get results. It is no wonder this organization doubled its multibillion-dollar revenue stream in three years after a decade of sluggish and sleepy performance.

CONFIDENT VULNERABILITY AT WORK

Imagine an entire organization full of leaders with confidence and a passion for learning and growing. These are teams made up of go-to leaders who can quickly *quiet their minds, notice* their thinking and actions, and *choose* the ones that will unleash their strategy. Confident vulnerability is undoubtedly a superpower that will fuel your culture transformation and unlock your organization's potential, leading to dramatic improvements in business performance, employee engagement, and overall health and well-being.

KEY TAKEAWAYS

- Showing up on autopilot creates cultures. Confident vulnerability allows us to notice and intentionally shape our cultures.
- Confident vulnerability is a way of being that increases leader effectiveness, the efficacy of transformation initiatives, and most importantly, the ability to deliver results.
- A healthy state of mind enables confident vulnerability and gives us the ability to grow and change, accelerating transformation.

QUESTIONS TO CONSIDER

- What are some of your personal autopilots that are healthy? What are some autopilots that may be limiting your effectiveness?
- Which of your team and organizational autopilots are healthy? Which autopilots may be limiting your team's or your organization's effectiveness?
- How often are you willing to share what you are learning, and what you don't know?
- What might be the impact to your business performance to have an organization of confident and vulnerable *go-to* people?

CHAPTER 11

FIVE ACTIONS YOU CAN TAKE RIGHT NOW

It's not just about hope and ideas, it's about action.

SHIRIN EBADI

We hope the ideas shared in this book have provoked you to consider your culture. The focus of this chapter is to share ways you can put your ideas into action—today.

We have distilled five simple, powerful actions that you can take to effectively leverage your culture to drive your business strategy:

- Notice your thinking and state of mind.
- Conduct a baseline assessment of your culture.
- Build your business case.
- Study successful examples from other organizations.
- Identify the right team to lead your culture transformation.

As we examine these five critical actions, a key concept will enable them all: developing confident vulnerability in your organization's leaders. We'll revisit this idea in more detail as we wrap up the five actions.

NOTICE YOUR THINKING AND STATE OF MIND

One way to notice more of the thinking within the teams you lead is to notice the language people use during meetings. The thinking could either be "I have tremendous influence on the outcomes we achieve" or "nothing I do will change this" or "it's not worth trying." For example, you may hear people referring to "the way we've always done things," "this isn't our job," or "they didn't get that to us." These can be powerful indicators of the level of IMpowerment within your team.

With regard to noticing your state of mind, try to step back and observe the body language and tone of those around you. Are people demonstrating healthy states of mind (confident, assured, curious) or unhealthy states of mind (critical, nervous, aggressive)?

A CEO of a high-tech manufacturing firm took the culture transformation process very seriously. The business environment in this company was dire. In both divisions of the company, prices had dropped to below production costs. The executive leadership team did not have a clear strategy on how to address the situation. But they knew dramatic changes were necessary to survive.

The approach they adopted was to *lead with culture*. The thought was that if the leadership team could improve the organization's health, it would be able to endure the tremendous change and restructuring needed.

This CEO started by simply monitoring his own thinking and actions. He noticed that he spent a lot of time blaming others and, as a result, his team blamed others and so on. Leaders would wait to be told what to do and would not independently take action or anticipate changes in the business. This led to very low levels of IMpowerment in the organization and a great deal of frustration for the CEO.

After he noticed this, he committed himself and the leadership team to operate from higher states of IMpowerment. He monitored his own thinking and states of mind. He asked for feedback from his direct reports. He took the transformation process, individually and organizationally, as seriously as any senior executive we have worked with. He asked, "Am I seeing my role in creating the culture—based on what I model, reward, and tolerate? How might I make an even greater impact?"

As his comfort and competence grew, he became a keen observer of the leadership team, observing how team members showed up at meetings and how their leadership reflections cascaded throughout the broader organization.

Finally, he monitored the organization to better understand what was going on there. He did this by talking to people, noticing them, listening to what was on their minds, and watching them interact. He was looking for indicators of improved organization health and effectiveness. He caught employees and leadership doing things right and reinforced the change efforts. He adapted an approach of doing what Tom Peters recommends as "managing by walking around." As this was an organization of 10,000 employees spread out over the entire globe, walking around had to be done virtually.

This CEO made it a point to reach out to employees and leaders worldwide to check in on progress. This included unplanned and unstructured meetings and discussions with people around the organization to monitor the organization's pulse. He would hear great stories but also stories that weren't aligned with the direction he wanted the organization to follow.

Rather than blaming and finding fault with local management, which would have been the autopilot of the past, he got curious and tried to figure out why things weren't moving according to plan and then addressed the issue with local management in a constructive way.

He took responsibility for everything in his circle of impact and was deliberate about his leadership reflection in shaping the actions of others around him. This approach led to defining solutions that moved performance forward. As a result, the organization not only survived this business environment, it led its industry in just about every financial and operational metric for the next three years.

Now reflect on your strategy and consider which behaviors are strategically enabling and which would derail it.

Today, like any other day, we are mainly operating from autopilot. All of the programming for our actions sits just out of reach of our conscious minds down in the subconscious. Quieting our minds will help us better notice ourselves and others. What is our thinking? Why did we act a certain way? What can we learn about our state of mind by noticing our feelings?

CONDUCT A BASELINE ASSESSMENT OF YOUR CULTURE

As you begin to explore your culture, it is important to know where you're starting from. It's also important to begin to identify how your culture is aligned with your strategy—both how it helps you get terrific results and how it is holding your performance back. We're confident that you already have a good sense of where your culture is today. However, it may not be intuitive to you at the moment. Let us share a brief story to help you quickly visualize your current culture and how it may be serving you or holding you back.

We met with the executive team at a large science and technology company to begin the culture transformation. We wanted to help them begin with their end in mind. We started by asking them to clear their minds, as we knew that being quiet-minded would be critical for them to better visualize their current culture.

After a brief exercise to clear everyone's mind, we handed out a blank summary diagnostic survey. In this survey, people could see the various dimensions that make up healthy cultures. They were asked to take a moment to individually identify those areas of strength and areas of opportunity in their organization's culture.

Once the team members had individually identified the aspects of the culture that were healthy and unhealthy, we asked them to turn to a colleague and discuss why they selected the items they did. Then, we went around the room and asked each executive team member to share the one strength, and one opportunity they felt was most important to either leverage or improve during the culture transformation. We took notes as they spoke.

After each executive team member shared their perspective, we shared the aggregate results on a whiteboard and asked the team for their thoughts. In particular, we were interested in exploring how their current culture was aligned with their strategy.

They quickly identified that a lack of entrepreneurial and performance focus led to a decline in financial performance for the ten years since the Great Recession. This new CEO knew at that moment that he and the senior team needed to get aligned on how to develop this performance focus in the organization.

Consider the metaphor of a *fire tower* in a forest. Well in advance of a detailed diagnostic process, you can get a sense of where to focus more attention by scanning the horizon for smoke. Using this simple approach, you can clear your thinking, visualize the culture, and align at a high level on what changes need to be made to enable your strategy—all in less than 30 minutes.

BUILD YOUR BUSINESS CASE

We were brought in to address employee safety in a large energy company. The president of a large division recognized that the work was being done with an unhealthy mindset. This unhealthy mindset manifested itself in three work fatalities, increased loss days due to injuries, and recordable safety events.

This experience, more than any other in my 40 years of professional consulting, proved to me that our mindsets matter.

A prevalent mindset was: "This is dangerous work and people are going to get hurt." This thinking was not just deep down in the organization, but all the way up to division leadership.

The CEO stated that he did not want to attend any more funerals for employees who were killed on the job. As a point of challenge, he pointed out how poorly this company was run versus other utilities. He then highlighted results in the chemical industry, also a dangerous field, yet so much safer than this company.

This company found that by focusing on several well-placed culture concepts, positive change began to happen very quickly. The most salient concept was having a quiet mind, being in the moment, noticing yourself and others, and being aware of the environment.

Safety became central to our language. In meetings, our work practices, and, most importantly, our thinking, we determined that zero accidents were possible. Lost workdays, recordable incidents, and OSHA recordable incidents dropped dramatically, and most importantly, fatalities dropped to zero.

This company not only went on to become an industry leader in safety, but experienced a number of "knock-on effects," positive effects beyond safety which include attaining industry-leading operational and financial results and other areas including employee engagement, being a great place to work, and employee diversity awards.

Safety will be the primary driver for some organizations in your culture business case. For others, it's about revenue, subscriber or account growth, customer focus, quality, etc. A large shipping company was about on-time deliveries and reducing damaged goods returns. For others, there is a focus on becoming a talent magnet, reducing turnover, and enabling leaders to effectively manage the future of work.

The key is to help the team and key stakeholders become crystal clear about the connection between their thinking and state of mind with their actions and results. Creating a consistently high-performing culture full of go-to people will drive tremendous results for any organization. What results will be critical for you to achieve?

STUDY SUCCESSFUL EXAMPLES FROM OTHER ORGANIZATIONS

Hundreds of successful culture transformations have been led by firms worldwide. Many of these firms have also talked about some of the best practices and lessons they learned in reshaping their cultures. Learn from them.

In many cases, you can hear from senior stakeholders, including CEOs, who talk about the critical lessons they learned and how they would approach their culture transformations differently going forward. And, in most of these cases, you'll hear that they should spend more time focusing on what is hidden in culture and less time focusing on what is obvious.

In a large grocery store chain, we were working with a relatively new CEO and exploring the need for some culture work. Throughout the initial discussions with the CEO, he asked each of us what we knew about his company and his culture, and what we thought about the store experience and the brand. He was gathering data throughout every conversation.

Once he believed he wanted to work with us, he asked for references. Once we provided references, he asked to speak directly with them and prepared a thoughtful set of questions for each of the references. He also asked for best practices, including podcasts and white papers on what leaders learned after going through culture transformation.

During this process, he learned what leaders wish they would've known before starting this journey, what they loved about working with us, and what they would do differently in working with us in the future.

It's so important to do homework and to be curious about the experience of others. There is so much information out there to help you begin to learn from others. We encourage you to go directly to the source, whenever possible. This means leaders of organizations like yours speaking firsthand about their direct experience leading culture transformation.

Taking this time upfront will help accelerate your culture journey and help you to avoid some of the roadblocks and derailers associated with moving through such transformations.

IDENTIFY THE RIGHT TEAM TO LEAD YOUR CULTURE TRANSFORMATION

First decide who, then what. As Jim Collins reminded us, the most important thing to do is get the right people on the bus.[1] While culture is not something you can delegate to a committee or HR, it is also not something you can tackle alone—especially in large, complex, and even matrixed organizations. You will need to identify influential leaders with strong *leadership reflections* and a passion for *what* you do as an organization and *how* you do it.

Clients often ask if they should exclude those who may be reluctant to change or have traditionally not focused well on the *soft side* of the business. *Absolutely not.* These leaders can find such a personal transformation to be tremendously energizing and inspiring. And, once they catch on, everyone who has known them (often for decades) is inspired to want to grow personally as well, and will follow their lead in transforming the culture by changing their state of mind, thinking, and actions.

As we worked through a culture transformation for a global consumer products company, we partnered with the CEO and CHRO to identify HiPOs, influencers, those on succession plans, and those with a long history at the company (and hundreds, if not thousands, of followers). As part of our work following the executive session, we assembled the top 100 leaders from around the globe to go through a culture transformation session at their headquarters.

At the beginning of the session, we started with the CEO keynote. As part of his keynote, he asked the Culture Leadership Team to stand and be recognized for their work in shaping the new values and leading the transformation efforts. You could hear a pin drop prior to the round of applause.

The Culture Leadership Team was made up of *the key leaders* and *influencers* across the company and once the organization saw who was leading this effort, they knew that it was critical to the organization's success, it would be successful, and they wanted to be a part of it. The CEO later told me that he *knew* his culture transformation would be a success at this very moment.

Who should be on the team to lead your culture work?

CONFIDENT VULNERABILITY IS THE KEY TO CHANGE AND CREATING RESULTS

Now let's return to the fundamental capability that will enable all five of these actions: developing more confident vulnerability in your organization's leaders. Vulnerability has been discussed, but the importance of true self-confidence hasn't been covered as much. As Harry Kraemer, partner at Madison Dearborn Partners, former CEO of Baxter Health, and professor at Kellogg School of Management, describes true self-confidence:

> More than mastery of certain skills, true self-confidence enables you to accept yourself as you are, recognizing your strengths and your weaknesses, and focusing on continuous improvement.[2]

While we develop an innate and general level of self-confidence over our lifetimes, there is also a specific self-confidence tied to your being in a healthy state of mind. This means that we are in a healthy state of mind, curious to discover and improve our culture through our actions.

At the beginning of the COVID-19 pandemic in 2020, one president of a U.S.-based consumer products company sat with her team virtually, trying to make sense of the situation. Their plants were idle. Their supply chain was disrupted, and employees were working from home. Yet, by the end of 2020, this division had its best-ever year in terms of financial and operational results.

The plants were running more efficiently than ever, the supply chain was re-configured, employees were successfully working from home, and the leadership team was more aligned than ever. What had happened during this very challenging crisis?

The president explains her team's experience this way. "We didn't know what to do, but we remained curious, open to new ideas, and humble, recognizing that we surely didn't have all the answers. With that said, we also never lost our confidence that we would prevail. We had tremendous experience and knowledge and a desire to win."

This leader and her leadership team were vulnerable. They kept an open mind, got curious, and questioned their assumptions while looking for new and better ways to do things. They were humble enough to listen to their organization members regarding how to invest and address the challenges. Rather than becoming a disaster, 2020 became the division's best year.

They were also confident, and with this confidence underlying everything they did, they knew they would be successful and would make a difference in the world.

This attribute of leadership is also spread across the team (and the broader organization) through your reflection on leadership. In a sense, this confident vulnerability is contagious.

KEY TAKEAWAYS

- Enhancing the ability to notice organizational culture is a critical step to enable cultural transformation.
- Determining culture's current and ideal states makes it possible to chart a deliberate course and get all employees on board.
- Engaging influencers in an organization is important to help generate buy-in and commitment from the broader employee population.
- Developing a succinct and powerful case for culture with clear outcomes will inspire employees to commit to personal change.

QUESTIONS TO CONSIDER

- What do you notice about the prevailing state of mind in your organization?
- How does the current state of mind encourage or impede the needed culture change?
- Is the leadership team clear and aligned regarding outcomes and how culture impacts results?
- Can each member of the leadership team consistently articulate a compelling case for culture? Why culture and why now?
- Who are the influencers in your organization that can inspire your employees to commit to personal change?

CHAPTER 12
APPLYING THESE PRINCIPLES TO YOUR LIFE

We're nearing the end of our journey through this book. Some of you might wonder how these human effectiveness principles apply elsewhere in your life. We're all whole people. Though we all might attempt to compartmentalize, it's our personal experience that we all learn and test ideas everywhere—at work, in the world, at home, and in our personal lives. In fact, most of us might even admit that family and extended family present some of the greatest challenges to consistently operate from a healthy state of mind.

We have seen how these principles can work in powerful ways at home, in our daily lives and greatest life challenges. In fact, we have heard numerous stories from CEOs and other executives as to how they took the insights they gained during this process home and made dramatic improvements there. We don't want to overplay this, but we've heard things like, "this saved my marriage," "for the first time in years, I spent quality time with my son," and "by being a better listener, I uncovered a serious personal issue that my daughter was struggling with, but not talking about."

So, as we wrap up, we thought, in the spirit of transparency and learning that we'd share two stories with you—one from each of us—that represent profound challenges we've faced, and how the lessons we've learned in the workplace have helped us at home, with the people we love most.

CHAD'S STORY

Can we really change habits that we've had for a long time? It's an important question to consider. Aren't the habits we have just the habits we have? Didn't we learn these as children and perfect them as they got older? Aren't they too ingrained to change? Here's an experience that taught me a powerful lesson about how dramatically people can change.

It starts with my brothers. I grew up as a middle child with two brothers, Kevin (the oldest) and Chris (the youngest). We were naturally very competitive with each other, often playing on opposing teams at school and in the neighborhood, fighting, and getting each other into trouble. I always felt that my older brother could do everything easier, faster, and better than I could. He was taller; a better trumpet player, athlete, and student; the youngest Eagle Scout in our troop; the first to join the honor society; and more popular. He was well-respected by everyone who knew him.

What I didn't fully appreciate is that while I was trying to live up to my older brother's standards, my younger brother Chris had to live up to my *and* our older brother's standards. I became a pretty good trumpet player, student, athlete, Eagle Scout, honor society member, and was popular (largely through my older brother's reputation) and well-respected (though not much taller for a while).

Chris followed along three years behind me in school, and I trailed Kevin by just one. All of the teachers referred to me as Kevin's little brother and, I'm sure, to Chris as the youngest Carr brother. Instead of trying to outdo Kevin or me, Chris quickly found that his coping strategy would be to rebel. He would earn an A one semester in a class followed by an F the next semester in a tough course—or find other ways to veer from the expected.

He started identifying and hanging out with others who would rebel against the standards set by their siblings, family, or society in general. Pretty soon, Chris was not doing well in school and was getting more involved with friends who were into smoking, drinking, and other recreational activities.

Ultimately, Chris graduated high school and decided to follow Kevin and me to West Virginia University, the in-state option our family could afford. But within one semester, he was rebelling against college and, ultimately, dropped out without many accomplishments to be proud of (by his or our standards).

Chris found solace and friendships with others who were rebelling and decided to spend time following the Grateful Dead around the country. For years, Chris was a Deadhead and enjoyed being a *part of that culture*—traveling the country with a group of rebels, seeing beautiful places, and experiencing the Dead's amazing music. And he continued drinking, smoking, and other mischief with his newfound friends.

To get by, Chris made quesadillas out of the back of his 1960s VW Bus with a pop-top and sold them to earn enough money to keep his dream alive. He moved from city to city, experiencing concerts with his friends. He stayed most nights in his VW Bus. It was the full Deadhead experience.

When I spoke to Chris throughout these years, which wasn't very often, he would tell me that I had sold out by working for a big corporation and that he was free to go out and see the world. This narrative served him well and protected him from facing his insecurity about success, which always involved comparing himself to his two older brothers and society at large.

When Grateful Dead founder Jerry Garcia passed away in 1995, my parents and I secretly hoped that this would be the end of Chris's odyssey and that he would do what would ultimately become necessary for him to do: to find a job that could support him now and in the future. Instead, Chris found other bands to follow until the late 1990s, when I distinctly remember having a heart-to-heart conversation with him about his future.

As I recall, the conversation began much as any other conversation we shared at that time, with Chris calling me a sellout and with me judging Chris about his refusal to acknowledge reality and get on with his life. After some discussion, I sensed more of an openness in Chris—a genuine curiosity to learn more about how I saw the world. It seemed as if Chris had discovered on his own that the path he was on was not sustainable and that he couldn't imagine a future for him unfolding from the way he was currently living his life.

As we talked and listened carefully to each other, I shared how I had elements of freedom in my life. I had the opportunity to take trips with the companies I worked for. Andersen Worldwide sent me to different countries to work and enjoy some of the local experiences.

I traveled to London, Paris, Barbizon, Toronto, New York, Chicago, Los Angeles, and many other places. And, with the vacation time and money I had earned, I could see many of the same beautiful parts of the United States that Chris had experienced.

I think that was when we first started noticing our similarities. And as I shared elements of my life plan with Chris, which included retiring early and traveling extensively, I could feel him beginning to consider alternate paths for himself.

But, after nearly 12 years of rebellion against any kind of job, much less job security, could Chris really *change*? He wasn't sure.

Although a new path was beginning to appeal to Chris, he wasn't sure it was as attainable. I approached my wife to ask if she would mind if I asked Chris to live with us. Luckily for me, she accepted him with open arms.

Chris moved in with us in 1999, and we quickly set up a system that was not about creating dependency but rather about helping him return to a path of possibilities that had always existed for him. We established what would be a fair rent to pay and helped him identify potential jobs he could have to support himself. Once he found his job, he quickly realized that education would be an important enabler for his future. He returned to community college just outside of Chicago to complete a two-year degree.

He needed a little money to get started, so we set up a small, low-interest college loan with him that he would need to repay in the future. With that, Chris approached college with a sense of curiosity that I'd never seen in him before. I always knew he had enormous potential, but I had not seen him apply himself like this.

When Chris got his grades back from his first semester of community college, he had a 4.0 GPA that he achieved while working full-time. He was as proud of himself as I was, and we quickly amended our student loan to be repaid on a sliding scale. For 4.0 semesters, Chris could deduct a significant portion of the loan amount he owed us. For 3.9 he could deduct a little less and so forth down to about 3.6. Below that, he needed to pay us back in full and with interest.

After just two years, Chris had earned an associate's degree and maintained his 4.0 GPA while working full-time. My wife and I could clearly see the confidence growing in him. At that time, Chris was working at the Arthur Andersen worldwide training center in St. Charles, Illinois. There he got to see professionals of all ages, races, and ethnicities from 80 countries moving through the spaces where he was working each day. He had new people to look up to as managers and leaders. As such, Chris grew increasingly confident that he could make a living that would be rewarding.

Shortly after graduating, Chris decided to move to Boulder, Colorado, a place he fell in love with while touring with the Grateful Dead. He quickly found a job there, and his confidence and curiosity led him immediately back to school to finish up a bachelor's degree in business from the University of Colorado at Boulder. He graduated with nearly a 4.0 GPA and was on the dean's list of the business school.

After earning a few promotions at work, he decided to return for an MBA at UC Boulder. He became a leader in his courses and with his study groups. He graduated with an MBA in just two years—all while working full-time.

As part of his transformation, Chris also gave up smoking, a 12-year addiction, and heavy drinking. He picked up running, hiking, camping, and bicycling. He became a natural leader and a tremendously positive and supportive family member.

Twenty years later, Chris is planning for his retirement and aggressively saving to bring that forward well in advance of age 65 so he can fully embrace his inner free spirit. Looking back, he would soon realize that he had the best grades in college of anyone in our family. He also achieved those grades while working full-time and made a more significant personal transformation than any of us.

I share Chris's story because it profoundly affected me and my understanding of personal change. We all know that this kind of change is not easy. But if Chris can make such a *dramatic personal transformation*, can't we, as leaders, be willing to make a small adjustment? For example, can't we:

- Start meetings on time more often?
- Ask more questions in those meetings to make sure all voices are heard?
- Share more appreciation when people work hard for us?
- Share more feedback in the moment with our teams?
- Spend more time in a healthy, confident state of mind?

No one is expecting perfection. We all make mistakes and will slip back, but with the support of others around us, we can make real progress that will create an entirely different organizational culture.

Chris's personal transformation story perfectly illustrates what it takes to change ourselves—even just a little. As shown in Figure 12.1, before his transformation, Chris thought that he could not achieve what he wanted: to support himself and be able to retire.

This thinking led to feelings of insecurity and an unhealthy *state of mind*. In his unhealthy state of mind, he chose rebellious *actions* and avoided doing what he ultimately truly wanted. And his *results* were living a less fulfilling life than he was capable of.

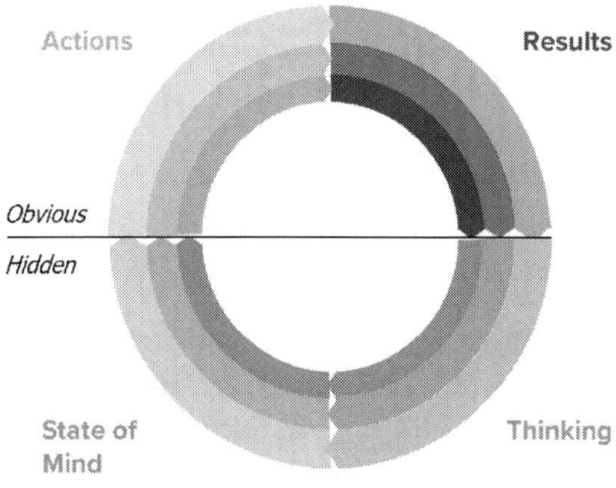

Figure 12.1 The Thought Cycle – our thinking creates our results.

What Chris needed to begin his personal transformation was to *shift his thinking*. With the *thinking* that he was capable of learning and needed to start by building a solid foundation with education, he experienced a more and more confident *state of mind*. He chose to *act* as a committed, capable colleague and scholar, and his *results* were remarkable, with rapid career progression and outstanding academic achievements.

In order to change, we must *be quiet-minded*

Here's the rub: we need to become more aware of the need to change. This comes from the ability, as author Ram Dass writes, to *be here now*—in other words, to be mindful.[1] How? Start by noticing yourself. From there, get to know yourself. This is your path to self-awareness. Think of this step as similar to learning how to drive an unfamiliar car. How do you start it? Does the car tend to pull to the left or right? How do you turn on the high beams? How quickly does it stop? Is the fuel gauge accurate?

Quieting your mind helps you notice things you hadn't really noticed about yourself before. It also allows you to notice more things about others. In Chris's case, he began to notice that he was rebelling. He then began to wonder if resistance to change for the better was serving him. He also began noticing that other, more productive paths existed for him— as he spoke with others, joined a new social circle at work, and became curious at school.

The more Chris took time to slow down and reflect, the more he could *let go* of the past—not to forget it, but let the past be *the past*. He started to notice his curiosity more and embrace it. Then, he turned his focus to notice what he needed *now* and who he was. This is how Chris evolved into a driven, compassionate leader with a powerful growth mindset.

In life, as in work, change can occur only if we see reality today, and that clarity comes by sustaining a quiet mind. Being in the moment and freeing yourself from distraction. Then, the truth emerges, having always been inside of you.

The next powerful lesson from Chris's transformation is the relationship between his *desire to change* and the *fear of failure* (Figure 12.2). We all feel this at times—wanting that next job, needing to change careers, eating better, exercising, or doing more for your family or clients. And yet, we have a counterbalance to naturally pursuing this change—the *fear of failure*. Imagine a balance where you begin to feel this desire to change.

What if we try something and it doesn't work? What if we aren't that good at it? What if we can't sustain it? What if we look bad? This negative thinking can keep us stuck and prevent us from moving forward. Only when our desire to change is greater than our fear of failure can we move forward through personal change.

Figure 12.2 The desire to change must outweigh the fear of failure.

For years, Chris woke up in unfamiliar towns, not always feeling safe and/or proud of his choices. He often wondered what other paths he might choose, but he let his fear of failure hold him back.

Chris would tell himself. "I never did well in school, and success there is required for success at work. I'm too old now to be a freshman in college. I won't fit in and won't be able to do well."

This negative thinking leads to unhealthy states of mind that produce less-effective actions and lower results. As Chris began to see success, it led to more confidence. And that confidence led to more success. The thought cycle shifted from a *vicious* cycle of self-doubt to a *virtuous* cycle of self-confidence. I'm so grateful that I got to witness such an amazing transformation. It inspires me and will be a source of strength and confidence for me for the rest of my life.

MATT'S STORY

One afternoon in April 2009, my 42-year-old wife Laura called me at work and told me that a tumor had been found in her colon. How was this possible? Laura was the picture of health. She was thin and beautiful, exercised regularly, and watched what she ate. Laura was having some lower GI problems and scheduled a colonoscopy at the request of her primary physician. We considered the colonoscopy as just part of a routine protocol. It turned out not to be.

Once the shock subsided, the first thing we did was research colon cancer. We read everything we could find online and in the library. We found that while stage 4 colon cancer survival rates were not good, stages 1 and 2 were very good. This provided a bit of hope on a very dark day. Surely, the cancer was in its early stages. She was so healthy. How could this not be stage 1?

At the time, I was working for a large healthcare company. The company's chief medical officer was formerly the CEO of a prominent cancer treatment center with colon cancer expertise. The chief medical officer put Laura in touch with a top-notch team of oncologists: a surgeon, a radiologist, and a chemo doc.

During the initial consultation with the team, it was determined that the tumor had grown to the point that it could block the colon. Surgery was necessary but was impossible because cancer had pushed into the cell wall of the colon and was dangerously close to an artery. Laura needed six weeks of radiation and chemotherapy to shrink the tumor. After that, if the surgery were successful, six months of chemotherapy would follow.

We were devastated. We had three children; the oldest was preparing to graduate from the U.S. Air Force Academy in less than a month. While we had many life plans, this graduation was something they had waited four long years to celebrate, and now even attending this a month out seemed impossible.

The next six weeks were very difficult. Laura was hospitalized twice after her colon shutdown, lost a lot of weight very quickly, which was concerning, and was unable to attend the graduation.

Following radiation and the initial round of chemo, the surgeon was very pleased with the outcome of the surgery. He was confident that he had removed all of the tumors. But he did find that the cancer had spread to nearby lymph nodes. This is never a good sign. The lymphatic system is the highway cancer uses to move around the body. This finding meant that the cancer was at least stage 3.

After several days, Laura was released from the hospital to recover at home but was rushed back to the hospital after an abscess formed in her abdomen at the surgical site. She was very sick and in great pain; she had trouble fighting the infection since her immune system was compromised by the chemotherapy. The priority was to get the infection under control, but this meant the second round and the more critical round of chemotherapy would have to be delayed.

After a couple of months of recovery, Laura was ready to see the medical oncologist, who would guide the next round of chemotherapy. She was feeling good and confident. Her blood counts looked solid, and she was prepared to fight this monster.

As the medical oncologist explained the various protocol options and risks, he mentioned that one of the scans suggested that cancer might have spread to the lung. However, a biopsy would be needed to confirm. A metastasis meant stage 4 colorectal cancer, one of the deadliest forms.

Laura asked the doctor very directly, "What is the prognosis?" The doctor attempted to answer in a somewhat ambiguous and vague way. Laura pressed, "What does this mean?" The doctor responded, "Stage 4 colorectal cancer patients survive between 12 to 18 months with the average right around 14 months. You are young and strong, and I would expect you to be at the high end of the range and likely live beyond those numbers." This number was consistent with research findings published by the National Cancer Institute.

On the way home, as our minds raced and our bodies were in distress, Laura turned to me and said, "Well, that's just bullshit, if this guy thinks I am going to miss Matthew's wedding, Amanda's graduation from graduate school, or Henry's graduation from high school, he's crazy."

Our son Matthew's wedding was going to take place in about eight months. That seemed like a reasonable goal. Amanda's graduation was less than two years away. That seemed possible. But Henry was ten years old, and high school graduation was eight years away. At the time, the National Cancer Institute did not even track stage 4 patients beyond five years because so few survived that long.

Laura survived for over 11 years, which was remarkable and against all odds. She saw Henry graduate from high school and begin college. She lived to see Amanda graduate with her master's degree and start a successful career. And she was there when Matthew completed pilot training, was promoted to aircraft commander, and finished his master's degree. Not only did she attend Matthew's wedding, but she also welcomed our three beautiful granddaughters into the world, and spent a lot of high-quality time with them.

Additionally, she continued to run her travel agency and made five trips to Europe, three trips to Hawaii, five trips to Alaska, and a trip to Australia, not counting the numerous stateside trips, including multiple Disney World and Universal Studios trips with the granddaughters. It was a full life for anyone, much less someone with stage 4 cancer.

Laura did not look sick. She did not act sick. In the last year of her life, she closed the travel agency to start a wellness coaching business focused on people with cancer and other chronic diseases. In fact, up until about four months before her passing, you would have been hard-pressed if you met her on the street to see that she was sick unless you knew her.

Why am I willing to share this obviously personal and painful story? To illustrate an essential point. My wife was an incredibly strong and courageous person. The stakes for her and our family were very high, but three overarching principles formed her approach to life and led to her success, which can translate into success in all areas of life. She gave new meaning to Jim Collins's belief that "greatness is about conscious choice and discipline."

The principles we have shared with you *work*. They are not only effective at work; they apply in life and death situations. I know.

I was there to witness Laura become a model of confident vulnerability and IMpowerment and put these principles into action through:

- Acceptance and focus
- Ownership and responsibility
- Appreciation and state of mind

Laura's first approach to life was absolute acceptance of her situation. She saw reality for what it was. The brutal fact was that she had an aggressive, deadly disease, but she also had goals she wanted to reach. She accepted what was in front of her. She couldn't wish it away. Laura dealt with this threat to her well-being and life directly by focusing her time and energy on the things which mattered most to her health.

Laura's second approach to life was absolute responsibility and ownership. She lived from a place of what we now call IMpowered actions, actions that come from within. She was determined to gather information about her disease and define solutions. For example, early in learning about the disease, she came across a story about the Harvard University zoologist Stephen Jay Gould in David Servan-Schreiber's book *Anticancer: A New Way of Life.*[2] Gould was diagnosed with mesothelioma at age forty.

As a scientist, Gould delved into the academic journals regarding the treatments and survival curves for different types of cancer. When looking at the variance in survival rates, Gould found that while, as expected, half the people did not survive past the median, the other half did, and unexpectedly some survived for a very long time past the median. This data dispersal is referred to as a right-skewed distribution.

As we investigated this, we were surprised to find that while the median survival rates varied widely by type of cancer, one pattern was very clear. All the variance curves were skewed to the right, which meant, similar to Gould's observation, that some people survive ten to twenty times longer than the median regardless of the type of cancer. The first question Laura asked was, "What are those people doing?" The second question was, "How can I have an even greater impact on my health?" Laura took full responsibility for finding the answers to these questions.

In reading the research, talking with survivors, and reading accounts of other survivors, Laura discerned several patterns of living far beyond the median. And while the programs, protocols, and approaches of the survivors varied widely, there were over-arching consistencies.

First was the importance of nutrition. Over and over in the accounts, survivors adopted organic, plant-based, whole food diets. Meat was eliminated or greatly restricted. In addition, survivors abstained from alcohol, tobacco, and almost all processed foods, especially foods with partially hydrogenated oils and high fructose corn syrups. Finally, survivors focused on micronutrients and phytochemicals in foods like cabbage, kale, mushrooms, and cauliflower and in herbs like turmeric and beverages like green tea to strengthen the immune system, reduce inflammation, and slow cancer cell growth. Making one of these changes much less all of them takes tremendous resolve.

The goal was to get the body the nutrition it needed to heal and eliminate all empty calories, which contain little or no nutritional value. This especially meant avoiding all artificially created molecules that the body could not digest. Also, controlling the food's glycemic index or sugar level was very important. Cancers tend to thrive in high sugar environments. Many of the survivors' approaches controlled the level of sugar in the blood.

Second was sleep and rest. A good night's sleep is critical for maintaining the cardiovascular and immune systems and regulating metabolism. These individuals went to bed at the same time and woke at the same time. This meant a consistent eight hours of sleep a night.

Third was exercise. Exercise increases the strength of the cardiovascular and immune systems, improves sleep quality, battles cancer-related fatigue, and helps reduce feelings of anxiety and depression. Survivors talked about a consistent approach to moderate levels of activity. The exact exercise did not matter as much as the consistency of an exercise regimen.

Finally, the vast majority of survivors had some approach to making sense of and finding meaning in life, and controlling stress and anxiety. Similar to what she found with diet and exercise, approaches varied in how people discovered meaning in life. For some, it was religion, for others meditation or yoga, and still others, nature or a connection to nature or combinations of these. The methods varied but making an effort to quiet the mind, find a sense of peace in the chaos, and give the body and mind a break from the stress was very common.

Laura found that positive thinking increases healthy states of mind. Such things as moods, feelings, and emotions become healthier and the body responds positively. She didn't blame others or wallow in unhealthy states of mind longer than she needed to. She quieted her mind, centered herself in her faith, and set a powerful example for our family and everyone who knew her as to how to remain positive in the darkest of times.

In all the above approaches, the focus on diet, sleep, exercise, and spiritual well-being, the goal was to prepare the body's immune system to fight cancer. But merely understanding these items is not enough. Laura had to take responsibility and possess the discipline to take action and to stick to the system she outlined for herself. It was a perfect application of the Thought Cycle (Figure 9.2). Her thinking about the disease and her ability to manage it was associated with healthier states of mind, which led to new actions and habits in the areas of diet, sleep, exercise, and spiritual well-being which created superior results in terms of quantity and quality of life. Her discipline and resolve were uncanny.

Throughout her journey, critical decisions about treatments and surgeries needed to be made. Laura utilized the same sequence of IMpowered actions repeatedly to get results. As the disease progressed, she would work to better understand the situation by reading and talking with experts. From there, she would identify options and define solutions.

Many of these situations involved experimental treatments and procedures that might extend or end life. In some cases, she would pursue the treatment. In other cases, and sometimes against medical advice, she would opt out of treatment.

Laura took responsibility for these decisions and accepted the outcomes. She didn't blame others and rarely second-guessed herself. She owned her disease and reminded herself that it was her life, not the doctors'. While the doctors were there to counsel her, she made the decisions.

Laura's approached life with deep appreciation. She was deeply spiritual and made time for meditation, prayer, and religious devotion. She traveled and danced and spent time with family and friends. She built two businesses and worked with her clients to make a difference in their lives. And while there were many tough times, there were far more good times. She remembered the good times.

It seemed to all who encountered her that she understood the true meaning of this quote from Irish playwright George Bernard Shaw:

> This is the true joy in life, being used for a purpose recognized by yourself as a mighty one. Being a force of nature instead of a

> feverish, selfish little clod of ailments and grievances, complaining that the world will not devote itself to making you happy.[3]

Laura was an inspiration for everyone and surprised many. In 2015, she visited an oncologist at another cancer treatment center after he published a paper with new research findings. As the nurse practitioner did the intake interview, she said, "There must be a mistake. This says you were diagnosed with stage 4 in 2009." To which Laura responded, "That's right." The nurse replied, "Wow, that's incredible. You look great." But she didn't ask the follow-up question, "What are you doing?"

This was not unusual. After years of meeting with hundreds of medical professionals, only two doctors asked, *"What are you doing?"* The first was a radiologist who responded to Laura's answer, "Keep doing that because obviously, it is far more effective than any of our solutions." The second was a medical doctor who practiced traditional and functional medicine and later became Laura's primary physician.

It seemed that the medical profession was generally not very curious about incidents outside their training or expertise or the established protocol. They viewed Laura's success as an anomaly or outlier rather than a learning opportunity.

While it is easy to criticize this profession from the outside, it is easy to see how similar things happen daily in our organizations. People with the best intentions are merely doing what makes sense to them. This is okay as long as the thinking is aligned with what is happening in the world around them. Once the world changes, we must ask different questions. Specifically, how often do limiting beliefs and established processes in our organizations slow or destroy transformational processes?

Laura's success at staying alive came from her willingness to define what was suitable for her. She listened to all the experts and then made a decision. Sometimes it was a traditional solution, and other times it was a non-traditional solution. She was not limited by certain beliefs, courses of action, or treatments.

In life and death, Laura gave me and our family the gift of life—she stayed alive for 11 full years after being diagnosed with stage 4 cancer and lived ten times longer than her original prognosis. She did this with a positive mindset, tremendous grace, resolve, and commitment to herself and us, her family.

Her courage continues to inspire me and has shaped my resolve to help everyone I work with choose to create healthy, positive, high-performance cultures and lives. This means understanding that we can overcome negativity, fear, autopilot behaviors, and mindsets with deliberate, intentional, and purposeful thinking and action. This is our mission, both Chad and Matt. And we hope to leave you with one simple challenge:

Create an awe-inspiring culture.

FINAL THOUGHTS

As Tom Peters began the book, *culture is the game*. It's the water we swim in. It's the fabric of our organizations. It can help us feel connected, productive, and successful and allow us to achieve awe-inspiring results in our professional and personal lives. And *you* own the culture *you* experience. Through your *reflection of leadership*, you create and reinforce the culture around you daily.

While the obvious elements of stated values, inspiring missions, clear competency models, and policies are critical, they are insufficient on their own to shape your culture. The hidden elements of building trust, developing healthy states of mind, and leveraging neuroscience will help you deeply connect and inspire others to bring your culture to life.

One bit of advice: If you start assessing, designing, and transforming your culture, do so by fully committing. Even worse than having an organic culture is identifying the limitations of your current culture, committing to make changes, and then failing to make those changes. It breeds cynicism and can poison the well for future transformation efforts as people quickly learn that such commitments come and go like the flavor of the month.

And, culture lives in our collective thinking, so changing actions without understanding the state of mind and thinking inherent in your organization will be an arduous and frustrating task. The key to personal, team, and organizational transformation lies in the hidden elements of *thinking* and *state of mind.*

We'll offer you one last moment to quiet your mind so that you can be deliberate, intentional, and purposeful with the culture you need to unleash the power of your strategy.

Take a couple of deep breaths.

Relax your focus.

Bring to mind what you truly need in yourself, your team, and your organization to advance your strategy and create an awe-inspiring organization.

Quiet your mind.

Notice.

Choose.

ACKNOWLEDGMENTS

This book wouldn't have been possible without the lessons learned from the wonderful leaders within client organizations and in organizations where we've worked. These inspiring leaders have helped us learn and test our understanding of how cultures work and are transformed. We are also grateful that Tom Peters helped pioneer this exciting field that we are privileged to work in—and that he took the time to write an inspiring forward that was a call to action to develop an even more compelling book.

Special thanks to our editor, publisher, and book-creation coach, Melissa G Wilson, for steering us through this effort. Without her guidance, this book would not be in your hands. We also had support from several writers, including Julie Anixter, Cheryl Booth, and Jon Malysiak. Julie's ability to blend voices and interpret some rather esoteric material was invaluable. Jon's ability to sharpen and reframe our thinking helped make this book so much more accessible for the reader. Cheryl quietly worked to refine our language so that it is intuitive. Illustrations were artfully prepared by Amanda Diamond and our cover was done by an artist named Mila. Finally, Gretchen Dykstra, our final editor, significantly improved the clarity of our stories and concepts.

We also appreciate Larry Senn—a passionate consultant, former colleague, and mentor who helped us learn a great deal as to how culture transformation works. Jim Hart taught us the value of focus and discipline and to be good at just *one thing*. Laura Basha helped us connect more deeply with the principles that underlie personal transformation and operate throughout our organizational transformation initiatives. Special thanks to Bill Parsons and Nick Neuhausel for being examples of how to connect deeply with clients.

Chad: I'm grateful for the support of my family, including my wife, Amy, who loves me unconditionally. My children, Brandon and Leah, have taught me a great deal about how these principles apply at home. My extended family is always there to support me in countless ways. And, I'd like to close with a special thank you to my brother Kevin, for helping me get Principled Transformation LLC started, and to my brother Chris, for showing me that personal transformation is possible—inspiring us all through the story shared in Chapter 12.

Matt: I am grateful for my time and life with Laura, whom I loved deeply and learned from much, especially as an example of faith, courage, and tenacity, and who gave me the three greatest gifts of my life: Matthew, Amanda, and Henry. I thank my mother and father, Jeanne and Ed, without whom none of this would be possible. And I am thankful for Kristi, who has been a pillar of love, support, and healing and has offered many fascinating perspectives and insights throughout the process of writing this book.

Finally, I would like to thank Jim Gilsinan and Bob Krizek, both of St. Louis University, for introducing me to theories and methods to understand and appreciate the concept of organizational culture in broader and more profound ways.

OUR GIFT TO YOU

Visit http://artandscienceofculture.com/bonus for links to this book's key concepts and models.

ABOUT THE AUTHORS AND PRINCIPLED TRANSFORMATION

Chad Carr, PhD, MBA, managing partner and co-founder of Principled Transformation, has a uniquely balanced perspective on culture, honed over more than 25 years of leading from both within and outside some of the world's largest organizations. After driving major transformations as a chief learning officer, VP of operations, and divisional HR leader at Fortune 500 companies such as Andersen Worldwide, Deloitte, Sears, and L Brands, Carr spent the last ten years consulting with hundreds of leaders to drive their culture transformations, most recently as a partner with Heidrick & Struggles.

The author of dozens of articles, book chapters, and books on leadership, learning, and organizational performance improvement, Carr is also a sought-after speaker, delivering keynotes and presentations across North America, Asia, and Western Europe.

Matthew Herzberg, PhD (ABD), MA, managing partner and co-founder of Principled Transformation, has been a C-Suite executive, consultant, and speaker. He has worked with thousands of executives in hundreds of organizations ranging from startups and nonprofits to Fortune 500 businesses around the globe.

Herzberg promotes individual and community health as a board member for the Herzberg Family Wellness Foundation (www.

herzbergfamilywellness.org), and the Midwest Health Initiative (www.midwesthealthinitiative.org). He is a volunteer for Boys Hope Girls Hope of St. Louis, an organization that believes children have the power to overcome adversity, realize their potential, and help transform our world.

The idea for **Principled Transformation** was born out of a singular purpose: *To empower leaders to create awe-inspiring organizational cultures.* This purpose statement has three highlights.

First is the desire to work with leaders to help them gain the awareness, insights, mindsets, and tools needed to guide organizations through change. For us, leadership is not a level in the organization but rather a process that anyone can employ to influence others to make a change, for the better, in the world. As Peter Drucker pointed out, "Change is the norm . . . but unless an organization sees that its task is to lead change, that organization . . . will not survive."[1] Leaders are the key to creating and sustaining high-performance organizations. Organizations that not only survive the tremendous changes in their environment but thrive.

Second is the desire to create awe-inspiring organizations, organizations that not only perform at the highest levels, but also are great places to work, places where individuals can make an impact, grow, and develop and be part of a team and purpose greater than themselves. Just as we look out at the Grand Canyon, the Swiss Alps, the Pacific Ocean, and night skies in the desert and feel an overwhelming sense of awe and wonderment, we believe the same can be created within organizations.

Finally, we focus on creating high-performance organizational cultures. Our experience is that culture is the true force multiplier in every organization. This multiplier applies to business, education, government, for-profit, and not-for-profit organizations. The culture embodies the collective thinking, thought habits, and mindsets that create a shared state of mind, including the organization's energy, mood states, and emotions, which lead to certain actions and, ultimately, business results (or lack thereof).

We believe (and experience) that leaders can create awe-inspiring cultures that yield sustained results.

We chose the name Principled Transformation because we believe there exist principles in the world that define individual, leadership, team, and organization effectiveness. When we adhere to these principles, we have effective change, successful transformations, and organizational results. When we violate these principles, we experience resistance to change, stalled transformations, and declining results. Our role is to work with leaders to identify, notice and leverage these principles in action to create healthy, high-performing cultures.

To live this noble purpose, we adhere to the following values:

- Be our best selves.
- Be client-obsessed.
- Innovate, lead, and learn with our clients.
- Be IMpowered to create outcomes.
- Value healthy differences.

We know that successful clients are the key to our success, but first, we must be our best selves. We must have positive energy and healthy states of mind to offer our clients the highest value. When this occurs, we can innovate and lead transformations with our clients, and while they will learn from us, we will equally learn from them. We work with our clients to gain understanding, take responsibility, and define solutions to create the needed outcomes and results. This is our concept of being

IMpowered. That is having power within to make a difference. Finally, we value and welcome the healthy differences people bring to the workplace, that is, differences created by background, heritage, personality, and experiences.

Principled **Transformation**
Unlock Potential. Unleash Results

We employ the colors of blue and orange in our logo. Blue represents trust, commitment, and confidence, while orange represents energy, action, and vulnerability. The logo has a stylistic "P" and "T" for Principled Transformation. There is also a more profound symbol. The first is that of a person illustrated in the inner circle. The person is critical to our approach since culture ultimately resides in the minds of individuals.

Likewise, the individual leader decides moment-to-moment the choices that they will make, thereby impacting the culture. The circle surrounding the person (the outer ring) represents the individual's awareness. This awareness allows the individual to ask the questions: Do I notice the impact of my actions on my performance and those around me? Am I taking deliberate, intentional, and purposeful action, or am I allowing my autopilot to run the show?

Finally, the orange part of the logo represents an arm. Just as sprinters raise their arms before taking off to increase their potential energy, leaders must prepare themselves and others for change and action before springing into action. But action is the goal.

NOTES

INTRODUCTION

1. Herbert A. Simon, "Making Management Decisions: The Role of Intuition and Emotion," *Academy of Management Executive (1987–1989)* 1, no. 1 (February 1987): 57–64, http://www.jstor.org/stable/4164720.

1. WHY ARE CEOS PAYING ATTENTION TO CULTURE?

1. Thomas J. Peters and Robert. H. Waterman, Jr., *In Search of Excellence: Lessons from America's Best-Run Companies* (New York: Harper & Row, 1982).
2. John P. Kotter, *Corporate Culture and Performance* (New York: Simon and Schuster, 1992).
3. Owino O. Joseph and Francis Kibera, "Organizational Culture and Performance: Evidence from Microfinance Institutions in Kenya," *Sage Open*, March 8, 2019, https://doi.org/10.1177/2158244019835934.
4. Jeff Bennett, "GM to Recall 8.45 Million More Vehicles in North America," *Wall Street Journal*, June 30, 2014, https://www.wsj.com/articles/gm-to-recall-7-6-million-more-vehicles-in-u-s-1404153705.
5. Emily Glazer, "Fed Rebuke Costs Wells Fargo About $29 Billion in Lost Market Value," *Wall Street Journal*, February 5, 2018, https://www.wsj.com/articles/fed-rebuke-costs-wells-fargo-about-27-billion-in-lost-market-value-1517858678.
6. Alex Edmans, "Does the Stock Market Fully Value Intangibles? Employee Satisfaction and Equity Prices," *Journal of Financial Economics* 101, no. 3 (September 2011): 621–40, https://doi.org/10.1016/j.jfineco.2011.03.021.
7. Daniel Goleman, *Emotional Intelligence: Why It Can Matter More Than IQ* (New York: Bantam Books, 1995).
8. Goleman, *Emotional Intelligence.*
9. David Eagleman, *The Brain: The Story of You* (Edinburgh: Canongate, 2016).

2. A FRAMEWORK FOR THE ART AND SCIENCE OF CULTURE

1. Charles A. O'Reilly III, David F. Caldwell, Jennifer A. Chatman, and Bernadette Doerr, "The Promise and Problems of Organizational Culture: CEO Personality, Culture, and Firm Performance," *Group & Organization*

Management 39, no. 6 (December 2014): 595–625, https://doi.org/10.1177/1059601114550713.

2. Andrew M. Pettigrew, "On Studying Organizational Cultures," *Administrative Science Quarterly* 24, no. 4 (December 1979): 570–81, https://doi.org/10.2307/2392363.
3. George A. Marcoulides and Ronald H. Heck, "Organizational Culture and Performance: Proposing and Testing a Model," *Organizational Science* 4, no. 2 (May 1993): 209–25, https://www.jstor.org/stable/2635200.
4. Peter T. Van Den Berg and Celeste P. M. Wilderom, "Defining, Measuring, and Comparing Organisational Cultures," *Applied Psychology* 53, no. 4 (October 2004): 570–83, https://doi.org/10.1111/j.1464-0597.2004.00189.x.
5. William G. Ouchi, *Theory Z: How American Business Can Meet the Japanese Challenge* (New York: Avon Books, 1981).
6. Gerald J. Tellis, Jaideep C. Prabhu, and Rajesh K. Chandy, "Radical Innovation Across Nations: The Preeminence of Corporate Culture," *Journal of Marketing* 73, no. 1 (2009): 3–23, https://doi.org/10.1509/jmkg.73.1.003.
7. Edgar H. Schein, *Organizational Culture and Leadership* (San Francisco: Jossey-Bass, 1985).
8. *A Few Good Men,* directed by Rob Reiner (Columbia Pictures, 1992).

3. MIRROR NEURONS AND NEUROPLASTICITY AT WORK

1. Dietrich Starck, Rolf Schneider, Hans-Jürg Kuhn, and International Primatological Society, *Progress in Primatology: First Congress of the International Primatological Society, Frankfurt A. M., 26-30. Juli 1966* (Stuttgart: Fischer, 1967).
2. Giuseppe Di Pellegrino, Luciano Fadiga, Leonardo Fogassi, Vittorio Gallese, and Giacomo Rizzolatti, "Understanding Motor Events: A Neurophysiological Study," *Experimental Brain Research* 91, no. 1 (1992): 176–80, https://doi.org/10.1007/BF00230027.
3. Christian Keysers, *The Empathic Brain: How the Discovery of Mirror Neurons Changes Our Understanding of Human Nature* (CreateSpace Independent Publishing Platform, 2011).
4. Roger W. Sperry, "Neurology and the Mind-Body Problem," *American Scientist* 40, (1952): 291–312.
5. Steve Kerr, *Reward Systems: Does Yours Measure Up?* (Boston: Harvard Business Press, 2009).
6. Norman Doidge, *The Brain That Changes Itself: Stories of Personal Triumph from the Frontiers of Brain Science* (London: Penguin, 2007).
7. "2021 Edelman Trust Barometer," Edelman, accessed February 25, 2022. https://www.edelman.com/trust/2021-trust-barometer.

4. IS YOUR CULTURE ACTUALLY OKAY?

1. Robert E. Quinn and John Rohrbaugh, "A Spatial Model of Effectiveness Criteria: Towards a Competing Values Approach to Organizational Analysis," *Management Science* 29, no. 3 (1983): 363–77, https://www.jstor.org/stable/2631061.
2. Brené Brown, *Dare to Lead: Brave Work. Tough Conversations. Whole Hearts.* (New York: Random House, 2018).
3. Carol S. Dweck, *Mindset: The New Psychology of Success* (New York: Ballantine Books, 2006).
4. Studs Terkel, *Working: People Talk About What They Do All Day and How They Feel About What They Do* (New York: New Press, 1974).
5. Shawn Achor, Andrew Reece, Gabriella Rosen Kellerman, and Alexi Robichaux, "9 Out of 10 People Are Willing to Earn Less Money to Do More-Meaningful Work," *Harvard Business Review,* November 6, 2018, https://hbr.org/2018/11/9-out-of-10-people-are-willing-to-earn-less-money-to-do-more-meaningful-work.
6. David Gelles and David Yaffe-Bellany, "Shareholder Value Is No Longer Everything, Top CEos Say," *New York Times,* August 19, 2019, https://www.nytimes.com/2019/08/19/business/business-roundtable-ceos-corporations.html.

5. HOW DO YOU BUILD CULTURE CAPABILITY?

1. Ayat Saleh and Richard Watson, "Business Excellence in a Volatile, Uncertain, Complex, and Ambiguous Environment (BEVUCA)," *TQM Journal* 29, no. 4 (September 2017), https://doi.org/10.1108/TQM-12-2016-0109.

6. PRINCIPLES OF CULTURE TRANSFORMATION

1. George Dixon, *What Works at Work: Lessons from the Masters: Personal Profiles of 27 Workplace Experts and the 10 Most Important Lessons They've Learned about People, Performance, and Productivity* (Minneapolis: Lakewood Books, 1988).
2. Rensis Likert, *The Human Organization: Its Management and Value* (New York: McGraw-Hill, 1967).
3. Robert Townsend, *Up the Organization: How to Stop the Corporation from Stifling People and Strangling Profits* (New York: Knopf, 1970).
4. "The Blue Book," Anixter, accessed February 25, 2022, https://www.anixter.com/fr_ca/content/dam/anixter/resources/guide/anixter-blue-book-en-us.pdf.

7. WHEN CHANGE SLOWS, LOOK FOR HIDDEN ELEMENTS

1. David A. Garvin and Michael Roberto, "Change Through Persuasion," *Harvard Business Review,* February 2005, https://hbr.org/2005/02/change-through-persuasion.
2. Kurt Lewin, "Group Decision and Social Change," in *Readings in Social Psychology,* edited by Eleanor M. Maccoby, Eugene L. Hartley, and Theodore M. Newcomb (New York: Holt, Rinehart, and Winston, 1947), 197–211.
3. Timothy R. Clark, *The 4 Stages of Psychological Safety: Defining the Path to Inclusion and Innovation* (Oakland, CA: Berrett-Koehler Publishers, 2020).
4. Aaron T. Beck, "The Past and Future of Cognitive Therapy," *Journal of Psychotherapy Practice and Research* 6 (1997): 276–84, https://www.ncbi.nlm.nih.gov/pmc/articles/PMC3330473/pdf/jp64276.pdf.
5. Peter M. Senge, *The Fifth Discipline Fieldbook: Strategies for Building a Learning Organization* (New York: Currency, 1993).
6. Ángel Lago-Rodríguez, Binith Cheeran, Giacomo Koch, Tibor Hortobágy, and Miguel Fernandez-del-Olmo, "The Role of Mirror Neurons in Observational Motor Learning: An Integrative Review," *European Journal of Human Movement* 32 (June 2014): 82–103, https://www.eurjhm.com/index.php/eurjhm/article/view/320.
7. Arie De Geus, "Planning as Learning," *Harvard Business Review,* March 1988, https://hbr.org/1988/03/planning-as-learning.
8. Goleman, *Emotional Intelligence.*
9. Eric R. Kandel, *In Search of Memory: The Emergence of a New Science of Mind* (New York: W.W. Norton & Company, 2007).
10. Doidge, *The Brain That Changes Itself.*
11. "What Is Neuroplasticity and How Does It Work?" David Perlmutter MD, accessed February 25, 2022, https://www.drperlmutter.com/faq/neuroplasticity-work/#:~:text=Alvaro%20Pascual%2DLeone%20recently%20stated,physiological%20changes%2C%20and%20experiences.%E2%80%9D.
12. Donald O. Hebb, *The Organization of Behavior: A Neuropsychological Theory* (New York: Routledge, 2012).
13. Humberto R. Maturana, *Biology of Cognition* (Urbana, IL: University of Illinois, Biological Computer Laboratory Research Report BCL 9.0, 1970), https://reflexus.org/wp-content/uploads/BoC.pdf.

8. HEALTHY WAYS TO OVERCOME RESISTANCE

1. Edgar H. Schein, "Organizational Culture," *American Psychologist* 45, no. 2 (1990): 109–19, https://doi.org/10.1037/0003-066X.45.2.109.

9. THE HIDDEN ROLE OF THOUGHT IN YOUR CULTURE

1. Eagleman, *The Brain*.
2. Herbert Benson, *The Relaxation Response* (New York: William Morrow, 1975).
3. Elissa Epel, Jennifer Daubenmier, Judith T. Moskowitz, Susan Folkman, and Elizabeth Blackburn, "Can Meditation Slow Rate of Cellular Aging? Cognitive Stress, Mindfulness, and Telomeres," *Annals of the New York Academy of Sciences* 1172, no. 1 (August 2009): 34–53. https://www.ncbi.nlm.nih.gov/pmc/articles/PMC3057175/

10. CONFIDENT VULNERABILITY, THE WAY OF BEING

1. Ron Carucci, "A 10-Year Study Reveals What Great Executives Know and Do," *Harvard Business Review*, January 19, 2016. https://hbr.org/2016/01/a-10-year-study-reveals-what-great-executives-know-and-do.

11. FIVE ACTIONS YOU CAN TAKE RIGHT NOW

1. Jim Collins, *Good to Great* (London: Random House, 2001).
2. Harry M. Kraemer, *From Values to Action: The Four Principles of Values-Based Leadership* (San Francisco: Jossey-Bass, 2011).

12. APPLYING THESE PRINCIPLES TO YOUR LIFE

1. Ram Dass, *Be Here Now* (Lama Foundation, 1971).
2. David Servan-Schreiber, *Anticancer: A New Way of Life* (New York: Penguin Books, 2017).
3. George Bernard Shaw, *Man and Superman: A Comedy and a Philosophy* (New York: Brentano's, 1905).

ABOUT THE AUTHORS AND PRINCIPLED TRANSFORMATION

1. Peter F. Drucker, *Management Challenges for the 21st Century* (Boston: Gruner and Jahr, 2003).

INDEX

Made in the USA
Columbia, SC
25 April 2024

34621284R00130